Freemasonry

Illustrated History
of the
Once Secret Order

Published by
Kandour Ltd
1-3 Colebrooke Place
London
N1 8HZ
UNITED KINGDOM

First published 2006

10 9 8 7 6 5 4 3 2 1

Author: Jack M Driver
Editor: Michael Vaughn
Design and Layout: George Georgiou
Production: Karen Lomax
Jacket Design: George Georgiou & Christian Nichols

Printed and Bound in China

ISBN 10: 1-905741-13-8

ISBN 13: 978-1-905741-13-7

FREEMASONRY

ILLUSTRATED HISTORY
OF THE
ONCE SECRET ORDER

Jack M. Driver

Kandour Ltd

contents

chapter 1

FREEMASONRY AS IT IS PRACTICED TODAY IS KNOWN AS SPECULATIVE FREEMASONRY AND IS ENTIRELY DIFFERENT TO OPERATIVE MASONRY, WHICH REFERS TO THE CRAFT OF STONEMASONS. HOW THE ONE CAME TO INCORPORATE THE RITUALS AND VOCABULARY OF THE OTHER IN ORDER TO DESCRIBE AN ALLEGORICAL SYSTEM OF MORAL SELF-IMPROVEMENT IS THE SUBJECT OF MUCH CONTENTION AND DESPITE THE ASSERTIONS OF MANY WRITERS AND SCHOLARS, NO SINGLE VIEWPOINT CAN CLAIM TO BE THE UNQUESTIONABLE AUTHORITY ON THE MATTER.

Shrouded in

Speculative Freemasonry went public in 1717 but had been pursued in secret for many years before. We know from the Reverend James Anderson in his "Book of Constitutions" that a meeting was held in the Apple Tree tavern near Covent Garden, London, in 1716 for the official union of brethren from four separate lodges, which had been accustomed to meet at the Goose and Gridiron alehouse in St. Paul's Churchyard, the Crown alehouse in Parker's Lane, the Rummer and Grapes tavern in Westminster and the aforementioned Apple Tree tavern.

There is even disagreement as to the original term Freemason. It could describe a mason who worked with freestone, which is a fine-grained limestone or sandstone, easily sawn through, but it could also refer to his status as a member of a guild, or the freedom to ply his trade in a municipality.

Most crafts were organized as local guilds, which set standards, fixed prices, controlled the numbers of new craftsmen entering the trade and set limits on production so that supply did not outstrip demand. As stonemasons might often work on cathedrals, abbeys and castles in remote parts of the country, they would operate outside the remit of a town guild and would thereby affiliate themselves to a lodge connected to the construction site.

Reverend James Anderson

Even in this arena of research however there is disagreement as to how mobile the population of stonemasons was. One point of view paints a picture of a largely itinerant population, moving from building to building, while another asserts that the larger building projects lasted sometimes for several generations and therefore there would not have been much movement.

What can be confidently stated however is that the use of secret words and signs which is so inherent in modern Freemasonry can be traced back to the operative stonemasons of medieval England.

The Regius manuscript, written in verse around 1390, details the history, customs and articles of the stonemason's craft, which was said to originate in Egypt. According to the anonymous author it quickly became

associated with the nobility as it was deemed an honest profession for second-born sons who would not inherit the family wealth and title. Supposedly it arrived in England between 924 and 939 AD during the reign of King Aethelstan, the first Saxon king to rule the whole of England.

The Old Charges, or constitutions, which it goes on to enumerate, regarding the conduct of a newly entered mason, are still in use in varying degrees in the rituals of modern speculative Freemasonry. Examples include the exhortation not to defame a brother mason's work but to help and advise on where he is going wrong, the proscription of adultery and the harboring of thieves.

The Regius Manuscript

Mystery

The narrative also contains references to Euclid, the Tower of Babel and the seven liberal arts and sciences in its discussion on the birth of Freemasonry and this has led some masonic historians to wild and unfounded assertions that Freemasonry predates Noah and the Flood.

This eighteenth century illustration has a reference to Pythagoras' Theorem at its center

Jacob

The use of a secret Masonic sign of recognition can be traced back at least as far as 1550 and there was even a designated officer, the tyler, charged with keeping the door to the lodge closed to "cowans", a Scottish word meaning "unskilled laborers." The emphasis on secrecy may well relate to the need to operate a "closed shop", that is to say, to prevent outsiders entering the trade and competing for business.

This version of the development of Freemasonry as a guild of craftsmen protecting their livelihoods does nothing however to explain the rise of speculative Freemasonry which has completely usurped operative Masonry. There are many theories as to how this might have happened, the most romantic of which involves the Knights Templar, and is dealt with in a later chapter. For the moment let us leave the middle ages and turn back the clock to earlier times.

To understand how something as seemingly uninspiring to our modern minds as the building trade became involved with a set of secret and heretical teachings necessitates an appreciation of the function of public building to the pre-modern mind. In an age of widespread illiteracy, ideas about the nature of the universe were incorporated into the fabric of Gothic and Romanesque cathedrals. In many ways, man was said to be made according to the same principles as the Universe and this four fold level of existence was mapped in the way the

cathedral was laid out.

The Nave represented the limitations of the physical world, which included man's material existence, the incarnate side of his existence.

The Choir represented the realm of the psyche or soul, which in medieval times included the abode of souls awaiting birth and judgement after death.

Further in still was the Sanctuary, the world of the Spirit and Archangels.

In the Tabernacle the Divinity was present through the miracle of the Eucharist.

Thus sacred buildings could be read even by the peasantry in ways that are almost completely lost to us. To go still further back in time, the masons working on the temples in classical Greece

Left: The ladder is an important symbol in Freemasonry. Here Jacob dreams of a ladder from Earth to Heaven as related in Genesis

The Square and Compass

various architectural styles in the orders of Doric, Ionic and Corinthian which, as we will see, play such a crucial role in the symbolism of speculative Freemasonry.

One of his overriding concerns was the way in which architecture could best represent the qualities of the deity to whom it was dedicated and really bring them to life for the worshipper. It is just possible that his fascination with the core of secret teachings preserved by the classical mystery schools, combined with a preoccupation with architecture, found its way to England with the Roman architects who arrived after the invasion in the first century AD.

It should by no means be imagined that every stonemason working on the religious and administrative buildings of the Roman Empire was a devotee of ancient knowledge and mysterious rites of initiation. However, there may well have been a core of well-educated architects with an interest in philosophy, religion and a classical concept of psychology.

When the Romans withdrew after the collapse of the Empire, the tradition may have continued in a kernel of secret knowledge passed on by word of mouth among like-minded individuals. Unfortunately, this is where theory broaches the arena of pure conjecture, because this is the era of the "dark ages", so called because the historical record is extremely patchy.

There was almost no monumental

and ancient Rome, and the architects of the pyramids of ancient Egypt would have been very comfortable with the use of sacred geometry, whereby principles of ratio and harmony that were so beautiful and universal in their application as to appear divine, were used to focus the mind and inspire both devotion and awe.

It is, therefore not such a great leap of faith from the use of sacred geometry (so essential to Freemasonry that the Deity said to be the source of all monotheistic religions is often represented by the initial G which is widely agreed to stand for Geometry) to create the perfect building to the application of allegorical geometry to perfect the individual.

One architect in particular who had a profound influence on the interplay of the form and use of a building was Vitruvius, the first to draw together the

The Arch of Constantine, Rome

building in stone for several centuries as the Saxons favored wood and thatch and the stonemason's trade disappeared altogether until the beginning of the eleventh century. However the line between the medieval stonemasons' guilds and the *collegium fabrorum* (the Roman architectural college) is easier to trace on the continent, especially in France.

As speculative Freemasonry is generally acknowledged to originate in England it is tempting to imagine that as the stonemason's trade died out in England, the link to the architectural past survived in the use of the tools and language of the stonemason as allegorical symbols which preserved the mystical teaching.

As the trade began to revive, the structure of the medieval guild could easily be assimilated to provide a method of organization and a smokescreen in times when heretical ideas were becoming more and more dangerous to openly espouse. This would be neither the first time nor the last that a seemingly innocuous group or trade was

Cathar Castle, in the Languedoc region of France

used to keep unlawful activities from the prying eyes of the authorities. At a time when adherence to Christianity was punishable by death, early Christians described themselves as fishermen and used the symbol of a fish in much the same way we use the crucifix nowadays. In the twentieth century, both the vocabulary and the infrastructure of the pizza restaurant business was used by the Cosa Nostra in America to import heroin from the Sicilian Mafia.

Bear in mind that this was a time when the Church was beginning to weld itself to the muscle of the state and insist on the cruellest forms of torture imaginable on anyone who strayed from the orthodox doctrinal line. To our modern minds we may imagine that the zeal of the militant arm of the medieval Church was directed at the stamping out of witchcraft and paganism and we often forget that far more dangerous to the authority of the Church were the schools of thought who differed only subtly from the traditional Catholic view of scripture. One of the most atrocious episodes in the history of the Catholic Church was the crusade against the Cathar heretics in the Languedoc region of France, in the thirteenth century, in which the famous words were uttered in

Robert the Bruce at Bannockburn

response to a question as to whom should be spared, "Kill them all. God will recognize his own".

A mystery school, with a classically-minded view of the spirit and the psyche, which promised its

Melrose Abbey

initiates a way to God that did not need the intercession of the Pope on one's behalf, would have been anathema to the Catholic Church. And this must go some of the way to explaining why Freemasonry waited until the power of the Church had been curtailed before it declared itself.

Dr. Robert Plot of Magdalen Hall

The seeds of Freemasonry may have come to British shores via another route altogether. Although four English lodges were the first to go public, Scottish Freemasonry is generally acknowledged to be the oldest form of the Craft.

There had always been intense enmity between England and Scotland, which reached a peak in the fourteenth century. Two factors may have contributed to the rise of Freemasonry across the Scottish border. Firstly many Templars escaping persecution on the continent fled north to Scotland where their martial skills would have been a useful addition to Robert the Bruce's fighting forces. Their contribution to Freemasonry is dealt with in a later chapter. Secondly, as Scotland looked towards France as an ally against the common English enemy, French culture became very influential, particularly in architectural terms and this can be readily seen in buildings such as Melrose Abbey. French masons may well have brought a core of gnostic

knowledge with them which was imparted with the use of teaching tools that would have made sense to a working man, in much the same way that Jesus Christ made use of agricultural symbols in simple parables to get his message across to the uneducated folk he wanted to reach.

If it did come to Britain from France, it had completely died out by the time it went public because it had to be imported back there at the beginning of the eighteenth century.

Cosimo 1 de'Medici Armato

As the punitive powers of the Church began to wane, Freemasons guarded their secret affiliations less carefully, hence we know from diary records that the famous collector of antiquities, Elias Ashmole, whose bequest founded the Ashmolean Museum in Oxford, was admitted to a lodge held in Warrington in 1646.

By 1686 membership in the Craft was so widespread that Robert Plot was moved to write in his "Natural History of Staffordshire" that the custom "of admitting men into the society of Freemasons" was "spread more or less all over the nation" and "he found persons of the most eminent quality, that did not disdain to be of this fellowship."

This quote provides a hint of what was happening to this erstwhile guild of stonemasons. Gradually the operative masons, that is to say those actually engaged in the trade, were dwindling in number to be replaced by men from the highest social and intellectual spheres of the country. Thus, when Ashmole joined his lodge in Warrington there was not a single operative mason left. These new converts were known as Adopted or Accepted Masons. The timing of this influx into the Masonic guilds of men from scholarly and aristocratic circles may be instructive.

In 1603 when James VI of Scotland and I of England came to the throne, the atmosphere of academic

John Dee

freedom, which had pervaded Elizabethan England since the Renaissance, changed dramatically.

Alongside the well-documented interest in classical learning, art and architecture, there had evolved an obsession with the Hermetic and Kabbalistic schools of thought which led to a popular revival of Western mysticism. Central to this revival was a blunder by the Church in allowing the study of a manuscript known as the Hermetica, which was purchased by Cosimo I de'Medici Armato in 1460 from a library in Constantinople.

The Italian monk who translated it mistakenly assumed that it was written at the time of Moses and thus prophesied the Messiah whereas it was actually written in the second or third century AD and thus represents a body of literature which would have been deemed heretical had the Church known otherwise.

At the same time, a great many Kabbalistic texts found their way to the cultural and academic centers of Europe with the expulsion of the Jews from Spain in 1492. Men like Pico della Mirandola were at the forefront of the investigation of this collection of mystical teachings.

The Roman Church was quick to put a stop to this dangerous trend in

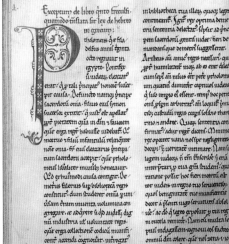

Fulcher of Chartres: History of the First Crusade, 1095 -1106

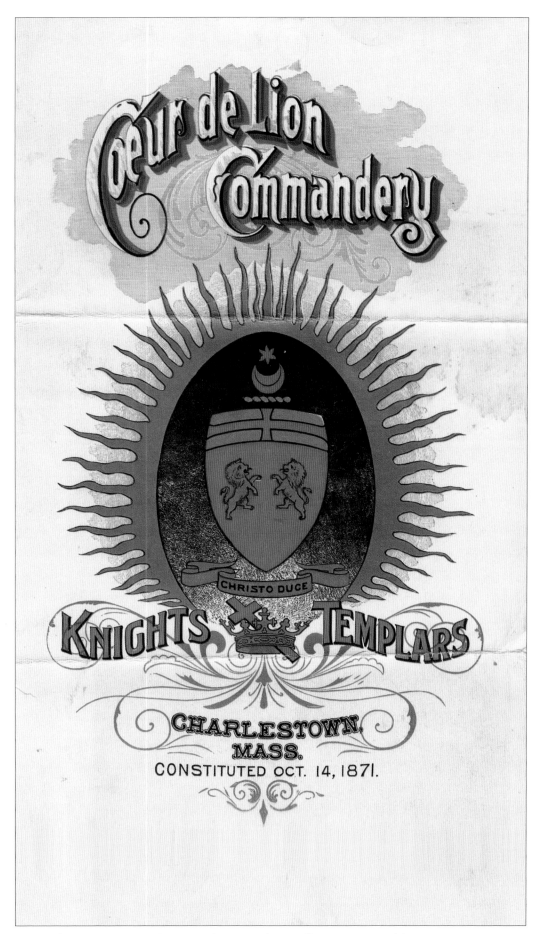

Coeur de Lion Commandery Knights Templars. A four-page pamphlet,
announcing a meeting at the "Headquarters" in Charlestown, MA,
on January 17th, 1893.

L'ACADEMIE DES SCIENCES
DEDIEE
Par son tres humble, tres obeissant et tres

ET DES BEAUX ARTS
AU ROY.
fidele serviteur et amie Seb. le Clerc.

Geometry and architecture are central to Masonic thinking. Humanity's progress in these sciences is recorded in this seventeenth century illustration.

Italy but its influence faded the further north you went and soon interest in occult studies, in the Netherlands and England in particular, was flourishing, the most famous advocate of course being John Dee, the mysterious polymath whose interest in the occult almost led to madness and certainly led to penury and persecution.

Interest in such studies and the subsequent suppression under James I and VI seems to coincide with the influx of accepted Masons into the Masonic lodges and thus it is not unreasonable to assume that men of learning used the Masonic guilds as cover to join together and pursue their interest in these ancient teachings.

Thus if we examine the records of the Worshipful Company of Freemasons of the City of London in the first half of the seventeenth century we find members "coming on the Accepcon", which refers to those new members who fulfil none of the requirements formerly deemed necessary to join a guild, such as the minimum number of years apprenticed to a master Mason, and is generally agreed to indicate a speculative Mason.

That the lodges had been operating a widespread underground network is evident in the speed at which the disparate lodges banded together under the umbrella organization of the Grand Lodge after 1717. From four lodges the number rapidly rose to sixty-three to include towns as far away as Bristol, Bath and Salford.

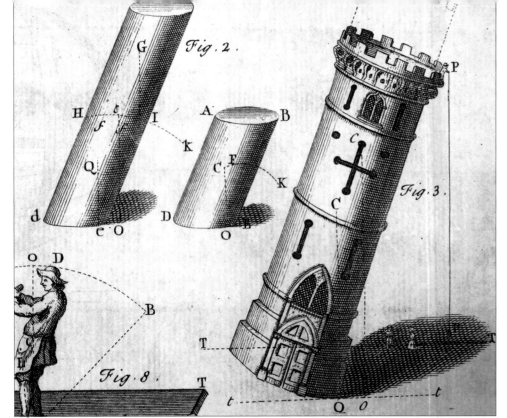

J.T. Desaguliers was both a fellow of
the Royal Society and chaplain to the
Prince of Wales

of Montague took over the role and by the beginning of the eighteenth century the Grand Lodge had been in the charge of the Duke of Cumberland, the Duke of Sussex and the Prince of Wales. In fact, over the next two centuries many monarchs were to join the brotherhood: George IV, Edward VII, Edward VIII and George VI of England, Oscar II and Gustav V of Sweden, George I of Greece, Frederick the Great of Prussia, Haakon VII of Norway, Stanislaus II of Poland, and Frederick VIII and Christian X of Denmark.

As early as 1719 an effort was made to collate the articles relating to the provenance of Freemasonry and by 1723 the "Constitutions of the Freemasons" was published by Anderson.

Even in its early public days the lure of Freemasonry to much of the British establishment demonstrates that this was no ordinary assembly of working men. Although there had been many operatives in one of the four original lodges, and indeed numbered among the first ten grand wardens were two carpenters, two stonecutters, a mason and a blacksmith, one of the other lodges was almost exclusively made up of the nobility and the officer class of the army and its master was the Duke of Richmond.

The spread of Freemasonry was not just through the ranks of the aristocracy, however; it rapidly established itself throughout Europe. Grand Lodges sprang up in Ireland in 1725, Spain in 1728, Gibraltar in 1729, the Netherlands in 1735, Scotland in 1736, Germany in 1737, Switzerland in 1740, Denmark in 1745, Italy in 1763, and Sweden in 1773.

The colonial nexus around the world ensured the global reach of Freemasonry, the first Asian lodge in Fort William, Bengal forming in 1729, and in Calcutta the next year. It arrived in the West Indies as early as 1728 on Antigua and was well established in Jamaica by the early 1740s.

As for the Grand Masters of the Grand Lodge, the first two were men of rather more modest means but the third, J.T. Desaguliers was both a fellow of the Royal Society and chaplain to the Prince of Wales. In 1721 the Duke

In the American colonies, Freemasonry rapidly took hold, with lodges opening in Boston, Charleston, Savannah, Philadelphia and New York in the mid-1730s. By 1734 Benjamin

Fénelon, Archbishop of Cambrai

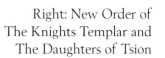

Right: New Order of
The Knights Templar and
The Daughters of Tsion

Franklin had been elected Grand Master in Pennsylvania and he went on to publish the first book printed in America with Freemasonry as its subject.

There were an estimated 6,000 Freemasons up and down the eastern seaboard and many of the most illustrious names in American history were members of the Craft: George Washington, James Monroe, Alexander Hamilton, Paul Revere, John Paul Jones, the Marquis de Lafayette, Benedict Arnold and Sam Houston, to name but a few. Of the American generals who have fought in the defence of America, Generals Mark Clark, Omar Bradley, George Marshall, Joseph Stillwell and Douglas MacArthur were all Freemasons, as were the following U.S. Presidents: Andrew Jackson, James K. Polk, James Buchanan, Andrew Johnson, James A. Garfield, Theodore Roosevelt, William Howard Taft, Warren G. Harding, Franklin D. Roosevelt, Harry S. Truman, Lyndon Johnson, Gerald Ford and Ronald Reagan.

Up until the American War of Independence, the lodges operated under provincial charter from the Grand Lodges of England, Scotland and Ireland but afterwards they set themselves up as independent and soon enough each state was governed

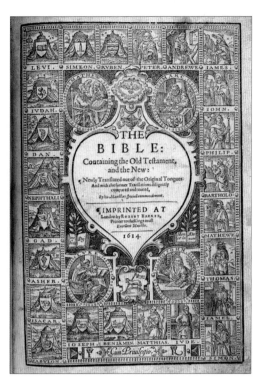

The bible is just one of many books that be can used as the Volume of Sacred Law

by its own Grand Lodge. Some effort was made to unite these independent lodges under a national governing body but without success, although after some co-operation on the erection of a George Washington Masonic National Monument, it was agreed there should be an annual conference of Grand Masters, which led to the Masonic Service Association of the United States.

It wasn't all plain sailing, however, and there were plenty of rifts, which looked set to spoil the image of harmonious brotherhood. In England for example there was some dissent among the disparate national lodges after the Grand Lodge first declared itself. Apparently there was widespread anger at the decision, taken independently and without any subsequent attempt at justification, to break the vow of secrecy. The anger was compounded by the imperious request of the Grand Master at the second Grand Festival in 1718 for all the lodges to hand over their historical records so that the Grand Lodge could draft a constitution. Rather than comply with the request, which would have made them complicit in breaking the vow of secrecy, many lodges burnt all their documents, which makes the task of tracing the origins of Freemasonry that much harder.

Several years later in 1725 the

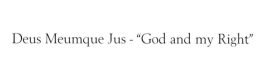

Deus Meumque Jus - "God and my Right"

Masonic lodge at York claimed that since they had a pedigree that stretched as far back as the laying of the foundation stone of York Cathedral in the seventh century they should henceforth be known as the Grand Lodge of All England, thus going one better than the Grand Lodge of England. It was not until later that century that their differences were reconciled and York Masonry came under the aegis of the original Grand Lodge.

In 1751 in protest at the Grand Lodge's divergence from traditional teachings and rituals, a group of Irish Freemasons in London formed a rival lodge and styled themselves the Ancients. For a while their influence exceeded that of the Moderns but by 1813 they too had decided to unite in the United Grand Lodge of England, which still has its headquarters in Great Queen Street in central London.

George Washington, founding father of the United States of America and an active Mason.

It was perhaps in France that the interest in Freemasonry developed the most rapidly. At first it seems the French were not very attracted by the idea of a fraternal society descended from medieval stonecutters but then all that changed with the arrival from Scotland of Andrew Michael Ramsay. With the help of the Archbishop Fenelon he became the preceptor to the Duc de Chateau-Thierry and the Prince de Turenne and in recognition of his services he was made a chevalier of the Order of St. Lazarus. This brought him to the attention of the father of the man who would come to be known as Bonny Prince Charlie, who brought him to Rome to tutor his son.

No doubt this illustrious pedigree helped when he later returned to Paris and set about advocating the cause of Freemasonry. He was the first to publicly endorse the theory that the earliest Masonic lodges were established by crusaders from the Holy Land. He gave an address on the subject, which went down a storm and won many new converts. Known as "Ramsay's Oration" it was given at the Lodge of St. Thomas in Paris in 1737 and described how,

"Our ancestors, the Crusaders, gathered together from all parts of Christendom in the Holy Land, desired thus to reunite into one sole Fraternity the individuals of all

St. Bernard gives the rule to the Knights Templar

On the wall of this eighteenth century illustration are signs for the lodges that started up since the Grand Lodge opened in London in 1717.
Note the square and trowel that several members are holding in their hands.

nations" and the association with Masons came about as a result of their desire to restore the Temple of Christians in the Holy Land. The secret signs had been necessary as "words of war which the Crusaders gave each other in order to guarantee them from the surprise of the Saracens who often crept in amongst them to kill them".

Lodges had been established in all the countries to which the Crusaders returned but had faded everywhere with time except for Scotland, whence they were now spreading over the world.

The kind of Freemasonry practiced in Ramsay's lodge was the traditional three-degree Craft Masonry, whose constitution had been formalized by the Grand Lodge of England, but his association of the Freemasons with crusading Knights took such a hold on the popular imagination in France that it spread like wildfire and soon lodges were competing with one another, awarding more and more degrees until it had been stretched to thirty-three levels of attainment.

This form of the Craft was known as Ecossaise, after the French word for Scotland, Ecosse, and it found its way across the Atlantic where it is still practiced today under the name the Ancient and Accepted Scottish Rite of Freemasonry.

In Germany interest in Freemasonry exploded after a romantic tale told by a German nobleman Karl Gotthlef, the Baron von Hund und Alten-Grotkau. He claimed that while in Paris in 1743 he was approached by a man

who called himself the Knight of the Red Feather. He invited him to attend the Order of the Temple where he met Lord Kilmarnock, Lord Clifford and a man who Von Hund later claimed was Bonnie Prince Charlie, the Young Pretender. They were told the "true history" of Freemasonry, which began when a group of Templar knights fleeing persecution by the Inquisition, arrived in Scotland and met under the cover of a guild of masons. Ever since their Grand Master was burnt at the stake, they had kept the tradition alive in such secrecy that the identity of the new Grand Master was only revealed after his death. This version of Freemasonry was known as Strict Observance because as part of the continued tradition of secrecy, an oath of unswerving allegiance had to be sworn to "unknown superiors".

Baron Von Hund was told to return to Germany, establish lodges there and await instruction. Initially the romantic elements of the story made this branch of Freemasonry extremely popular but as it became apparent that no further revelations were forthcoming the movement died out and Von Hund went to his grave still waiting to be contacted.

There are several theories as to the explanation of this story. One is that Strict Observance Freemasonry was a front organization for the Jacobite cause and that the reason Von Hund was never contacted again was the defeat of the Jacobites at Culloden in 1746. Another, equally romantic, is that they were a branch of the shadowy Priory of Sion, which was brought to world-wide attention by the books "The Holy Blood and the Holy Grail" and more recently Dan Brown's "The Da Vinci Code".

Such romantic mysteries connected to Freemasonry led to ever more evocative and illustrious titles for emergent lodges. Some of the most impressive are The International Order of the Eastern Star, The Red Cross of Constantine, The Mystic Order of Veiled Prophets of the Enchanted Realm, The Tall Cedars of Lebanon, and of course The Ancient Arabic Order of the Nobles of the Mystic Shrine, which is better known nowadays as the "Shriners".

Names such as these and various impressive origins that many early Masonic historians proposed for Freemasonry amongst the Israelites, ancient Egyptians, Essenes, Zoroastrians, Chaldeans, Phoenicians and Celtic Druids, lent Freemasonry an exotic lure which many writers, artists and musicians were unable to resist. Men such as Mozart, Haydn, Sibelius, Gilbert and Sullivan, Sir Walter Scott, Robert Burns, Rudyard Kipling, Jonathan Swift, Oscar Wilde, Mark Twain and Sir Arthur Conan Doyle lent the brotherhood an air of glamor which in turn attracted lesser mortals.

The humble guild of stonecutters had gone global.

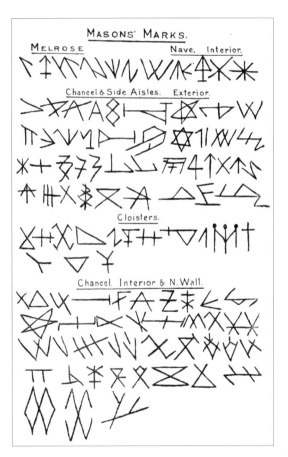

A collection of ciphers made by the stonemasons who built Melrose Abbey

chapter 2

ONCE A CANDIDATE HAS BEEN INVITED TO ENTER THE MASONIC ORDER, HE IS INITIATED INTO THE FIRST DEGREE AS AN ENTERED APPRENTICE MASON, WHICH IS ALSO REFERRED TO AS THE GROUND FLOOR OF SOLOMON'S TEMPLE. IN THE EARLY DAYS AFTER FREEMASONRY DECLARED ITSELF TO THE WORLD, THE CEREMONY WOULD HAVE BEEN HELD IN ROOMS FOR HIRE, PERHAPS ABOVE A TAVERN, AND ALL THE ACCOUTREMENTS WOULD HAVE BEEN TEMPORARY.

THE SYMBOLS ON THE FLOOR FOR EXAMPLE, SUCH AS THE CIRCLE, THE COMPASS AND SQUARE WOULD HAVE BEEN DRAWN IN CHALK AND THE ENTERED APPRENTICE GIVEN A MOP AND BUCKET TO WIPE AWAY ALL TRACES WHEN THE CEREMONY WAS FINISHED.

An elaborately marked sword of a type
used in the initiation of a Master Mason

Entered Apprentice

Rituals and

Nowadays, with the need for secrecy gone, Masonic symbolism can be intricately and lavishly wrought as the permanent fixtures of an established lodge.

Before the ceremony can proceed, a final interrogation takes place, in which the motives of the candidate for seeking membership are drawn out. A desire to exploit the connections of the Freemasons disqualifies a candidate for membership. Rather he must express a wish to perfect himself through the acquisition of knowledge and charitable acts towards his fellow man.

If all goes well, the next stage is for the candidate to strip the left side of his body. Nowadays, a special costume is supplied, with a shoe for the right foot but originally the candidate would have rolled the left trouser leg above the knee and removed the left shoe,

and he would have slipped his left arm out of his shirt, baring the chest and shoulder.

He is then divested of all metal objects, "hoodwinked", which means blindfolded and a rope called a cable-tow is draped around the neck so that the ends trail on the floor.

The Worshipful Master will ask the Junior Deacon the first care of a Mason and he will reply,

"To see the Lodge tyled, Worshipful".

"Attend to that part of your duty", the Master tells

King Solomon's Temple within the walls of Jerusalem, until destroyed by the Babylonians 400 years after it was built

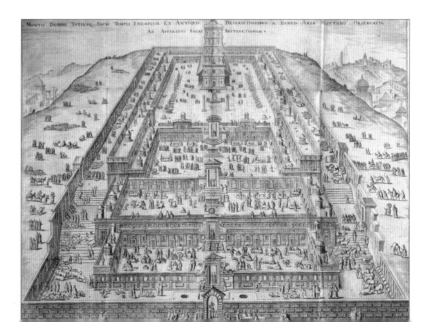

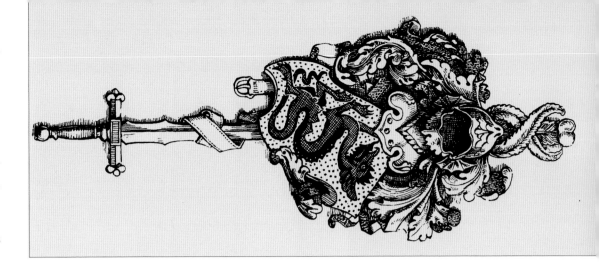

him, "and inform the Tyler that we are about to open a Lodge of Entered Apprentice Masons, and direct him to tyle accordingly."

When the Junior Deacon reports that the door is tyled, the Master asks "By whom?" and the reply is,

"By a Master Mason outside the door, armed with the proper implement of his office".

The proper implement is always a ceremonial sword.

"His duty there?" is the next question.

"To keep off all cowans and eavesdroppers, and to see that none pass or repass without permission from the Chair."

the Senior Deacon, waiting with the ceremonial compass in his hand. He presses the tip of the compass into his chest with the words,

"Mr ____, upon your entering this lodge for the first time I receive you on the point of a sharp instrument pressing into your naked left breast, which is to teach you that as it is a torture to your flesh, so should the recollection of it ever be to your mind and conscience, should you attempt to reveal the secrets of Masonry unlawfully".

Initiation

A cowan is a Scottish word which in this instance means a working but unqualified stonemason and hence is used to describe an intruder in a Masonic lodge.

Then each officer is identified along with his role, and the Master gives the signs of the degree to which the initiate is to be entered. Everyone present except for the candidate must give the sign to show that they have a right to be there. The lodge is now open and the candidate is led blindfolded by the Junior Deacon to

As they are about to pass around the room, the Master stops the Senior Deacon to remind him that a journey of such import must first partake of the blessings of God. A prayer is then offered, in which the candidate dedicates himself to the service of God and the brotherhood.

The question is then asked, "In whom do you put your trust?" and the reply "In God" is given.

Now the journey around the room may begin. When they come to the Junior Warden, he demands to know

1. Le Grand Maître.
2. l'Orateur.
3. le Secretaire.
4.5.6. Freres aux Rouleaux
    de papier.
7. le premier Surveillant.

Assemblée de Francs-Maçor

Entrée du Reçi

Dedié au très Galant, très sincere et très veridique Frere p

ur la Reception des Maitres.
ire dans la Loge.

Leonard Gabanon, Auteur du Catechisme des Francs-Maçons.

8. le second Surveillant.
9. le Tresorier.
10. le Frere Sentinelle.
11. Recipiendaire entrant dans la Loge.
12. Recipiendaire a qui le Grand Maitre
    n'a pas encore donné l'acollade.

The murder of Hiram Abiff
is central to the ritual of the
Third Degree

The fabric apron of a Master Mason, with dark blue cloth fringe; painted emblem and red bunting outline on round flap, c 1780

who has come to him.

"Mr _____" is the reply, "who has long been in darkness and now seeks to be brought to Light and to receive the rights and benefits of this Worshipful Lodge, erected to God and dedicated to the holy Saint John, as all brothers have done before."

There follow questions to ascertain his fitness and reasons for wanting initiation. Then he is led to the station of the Senior Deacon, where he is questioned along the same lines, prior to being taken before the Senior Deacon. The questions and answers exchanged here are essentially the same, only when the Master asks "From whence come you, and whither are you travelling?" the Senior Deacon answers for him,

"From the West, and travelling towards the East".

"Why leave you the West and travel towards the East?"

"In search of Light."

At this point, the Master asks that the initiate be taken to the Senior Warden in the east so that he may instruct him how to approach. When they both arrive at the altar, the Senior Warden positions the heel of the candidate's right foot so that it rests against the hollow of the left foot at a right angle.

The Master now leaves his station in the east and proceeds to the altar where he tells the candidate that he can go no further

until he has taken a "solemn oath and obligation" which though binding will not interfere with his duties to God, his country, his family or his friends. He must then assume the position to take the oath, which is kneeling with his right leg out and his weight supported on his bare left knee. His left palm goes under the book of his chosen faith, which is open on the altar before him, with the compass and square resting on top (the square above the compass). His right palm rests on top of the compass and square and he repeats the oath of the Entered Apprentice.

"I, _____, of my own free will and accord, in the presence of Almighty God, and this Worshipful Lodge erected to Him, and dedicated to the holy Saint John, do hereby and hereon most sincerely promise and swear that I will always hail, ever conceal and never reveal, any of the arts, parts or points of the hidden mysteries of ancient Freemasonry which may have been, or hereafter shall be, at this time, or any future period, communicated to me as such, to any person or persons whomever, except it be to a true and lawful brother Mason, or in a regularly constituted lodge of Masons; nor unto him or them until by strict trial, due examination, or lawful information I shall have found him, or them, as lawfully entitled to the same as I am myself. I furthermore promise and swear that I will not print, paint, stamp, stain, cut, carve, mark, or engrave them, to cause the same to be done on anything movable or immovable, capable of receiving the least impression of a word, syllable, letter, or

Cuff link: This example of masonic handicraft represents a time when masonic jewellery—not to be confused with masonic regalia—was hard to come by in the North American West.

It was not uncommon for Freemasons of a creative flair to design their own regalia, lodge furnishings and such items of personal jewellery or ornamentation.

Satin apron. English: c 1800

character, whereby the same may become legible or intelligible to any person under the canopy of heaven, and the secrets of Masonry thereby unlawfully obtained through my unworthiness.

"All this I most solemnly, sincerely promise and swear, with a firm and steadfast resolution to perform the same, without any mental reservation or secret evasion of mind whatever, binding myself under no less penalty than that of having my throat cut across, my tongue torn out by its roots, and my body buried in the rough sands of the sea, at low-water mark, where the tide ebbs and flows twice in twenty-four hours, should I ever knowingly violate this my Entered Apprentice obligation. So help me God, and keep me steadfast in the due performance of the same."

To seal the oath, the candidate kisses the book of his faith and is then asked what it is that he seeks above all else, to which he answers "Light".

At this, his blindfold is removed to signify his leaving the world of spiritual darkness and entering the realm of enlightenment. He is taught the handgrip and two hand signs of the Entered Apprentice, the "penal sign" and the "due-guard". The former recalls the punishment for revealing the secrets of Freemasonry, as the hand, thumb inward, is drawn across the throat in a slicing motion and then dropped to the side. The latter adopts the same position as when the book was held, the hands a couple of inches apart, with the right palm down and the left palm up.

Grand Sword Bearer collar jewel. c 1872

There follows the presentation of the apron, which was once a white lambskin, but is now usually white cloth or felt, either plain or decorated with Masonic symbols, according to the tradition of the individual lodge. This apron, he is told, is a symbol of innocence "more ancient than the Golden Fleece or the Roman Eagle" and he is shown the manner in which it was first worn by the Entered Apprentices at the building of the Temple of Solomon.

Just when the initiate thinks the ceremony might finally be over, the Master asks him to contribute something metallic, no matter how small to the lodge. Remembering that he was divested of all metal objects at the beginning of the ceremony, he is naturally confused and incapable of acceding to the request. The Master dispels his confusion by telling him that he has nothing of value about his person, he is utterly destitute, and he must be heedful of this memory if he ever comes across a friend or brother Mason in a like condition. Should he do so he is to give as generously as he can, according to the need, but making sure that in doing so, he does not risk material injury to himself or to his family. Thus the charitable side of Freemasonry is impressed upon him.

To end the ceremony, the initiate is presented with the "working tools of an Entered Apprentice": the twenty-four-inch gauge, which symbolizes the division to allow for periods of work, refreshment,

The cuffs at the top are those of the District Grand Master of British Columbia. The second pair of cuffs are those of a Deputé Master (the Square and Compasses combined). The use of thistles as well as the general design and color is Scottish.

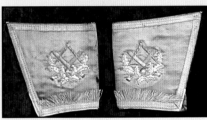

Master Masons' Jewels

sleep and acts of charity, and the gavel used symbolically to chip away vice and triviality from the Mason's character, so that he may shape himself into a perfect ashlar stone, suitable to take his place in the temple of God.

FELLOW CRAFT

The second level of initiation in Craft Masonry is that of the Fellow Craft. There is some speculation among

writers on Freemasonry that originally the second degree was the final degree and the third degree of Master Mason was a relatively late addition to the hierarchy, the title Master denoting a Master of a particular lodge, and not of a higher level of initiation.

In this ceremony the right side of the body rather than the left is revealed with the chest, leg and foot laid bare. The cable-tow is looped twice around the neck and the candidate is blindfolded. Nowadays a blindfold is

used, but in the days before Freemasonry declared itself in 1717 a hood was pulled down over the eyes, which explains the use of the falconry term "hoodwink".

Although this is essentially a prop to add drama to the proceedings, it would once have been a crucial element of admitting someone to a secret society. After all, if the initiate saw the members' faces before he had taken the oath of secrecy, it could have spelled disaster for everyone present.

When the candidate reaches the altar after being guided around the room he is placed in the position he must assume to make his oath. He kneels on his right knee, his right hand on the compass and square which rest on his book of faith, his left hand raised in the air, with his forearm and upper arm making a right angle at the crook of the elbow.

Variations on the Square and Compasses

And then he repeats after the Master,

"I,____, of my own free will and accord, in the presence of Almighty God and this Worshipful Lodge of Fellow Craft Masons, erected to God and dedicated to the holy Saint John, do hereby and hereon most solemnly promise and swear, in addition to my former obligation, that I will not give the secrets of the degree of a Fellow Craft Mason to anyone of an inferior degree, nor to any other being in the known world, except it be to a true

obey all regular signs and summonses given, handed, sent, or thrown to me by the hand of a brother Fellow Craft Mason, or from the body of a just and lawfully constituted lodge of such; provided it be within the length of my cable-tow, or a square and angle of my work. Furthermore do I promise and swear that I will aid and assist all poor and penniless brethren Fellow Crafts, their widows and orphans, wheresoever disposed around the globe, they applying to me as such, as far as in my power

  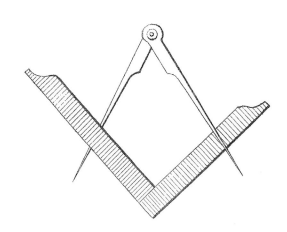

and lawful brother or brethren Fellow Craft Masons, or within the body of a just and lawfully constituted lodge of such; and not unto him nor unto them whom I only hear to be so to be, after strict trial and due examination, or lawful information. Furthermore, I do promise and swear that I will not knowingly harm this lodge, nor a brother of this degree myself, nor suffer it to be done by others, if in my power to prevent it.

"Furthermore do I promise and swear that I will

without injuring myself and family. To all of which I most solemnly and sincerely promise and swear without the least hesitation, mental reservation, or self-evasion of mind in me whatever, binding myself under no less penalty than to have my left breast torn open and my heart and vitals taken from thence and thrown over my left shoulder and carried into the valley of Jehosaphat, there to become a prey to the wild beasts of the field and the wild vultures of the air, if ever I should prove wilfully guilty of violating any part of this my solemn oath or

The "G" and the All-seeing Eye
are interchangeable

1. *Le Grand Maître*.
2. *le p.r Surveillant*.
3. *le 2.e Surveillant*.
4. *le Recipiendaire*
   couché sur le Cercueil.

Assemblée de Francs-Maçons
Le Recipiendaire est couché sur le Cercueil dessin
Et tous les assistans ayant tiré
Dedié au très Galant, très sincere et très veridique Frere

ur la Reception des Maitres.
s la Loge, le visage couvert d'un linge teint de sang.
luy presentent la pointe au Corps
Leonard Gabanon, Auteur du Catechisme des Francs-Macons.

5.6.7. Recipiendaires
a qui le Grand
Maitre n'a pas
encore donné
l'acollade.

The candidate's face is
covered while swords
are pointed at his body.
He is then raised after a
symbolic death.

obligation of a Fellow Craft Mason, so help me God, and keep me steadfast in the performance of the same."

Safe in the knowledge that the initiate has vowed not to reveal the secrets of Freemasonry, the blindfold can now be removed. He learns the new handgrips, passwords, penal sign and due-guard. This last has the hands in the same position as when the oath was taken. To perform

the penal sign, the right hand is moved across the left breast and then falls to the side.

Depending on how wealthy the lodge is the initiate is then shown either a real or a figurative spiral staircase that leads to the Middle Chamber of the Temple of Solomon. On either side of the staircase are two columns

Initiation of an Apprentice.

which recall Jachin and Boaz, the huge bronze columns that stood over the outer porch of the Temple. According to Masonic legend the columns were hollow and inside them, safe from flood and fire, were the documents of arcane lore and spiritual truths which the Freemasons were entrusted to guard. Atop both columns is a globe, one representing the Earth and the other the Heavens.

Contemplating these globes, the initiate is reminded of the importance of the study of astronomy, navigation and geography. At this point he is also told that whereas Operative Masonry was responsible for the building of many of the world's most famous architectural triumphs, such as the Temple of Solomon, the purpose of Speculative Masonry, or Allegorical Masonry, is the perfection of Man.

The first three steps of the spiral staircase, as well as representing Wisdom, Strength and Beauty, stand for the three ages of Youth, Manhood and Old Age. For a Mason, they correspond to Entered Apprentice, Fellow Craft and Master Mason. The period he is now entering should be a time of the ripening of the fruits of his studies, as knowledge broadens out into wisdom. Good works and charity will ensure his passage onto the degree of Master Mason, when he will be able to reflect on a good life, confidant of eternal peace and harmony with his Maker.

The next five steps represent both the five senses of sight, smell, touch, hearing and taste, as well as the five orders of architecture: Doric, Ionic, Tuscan, Corinthian and Composite.

The next seven steps stand for a number of septets: the seven years it took to build the Temple of Solomon,

The moon was given graphic and ritualistic importance by the medieval alchemists

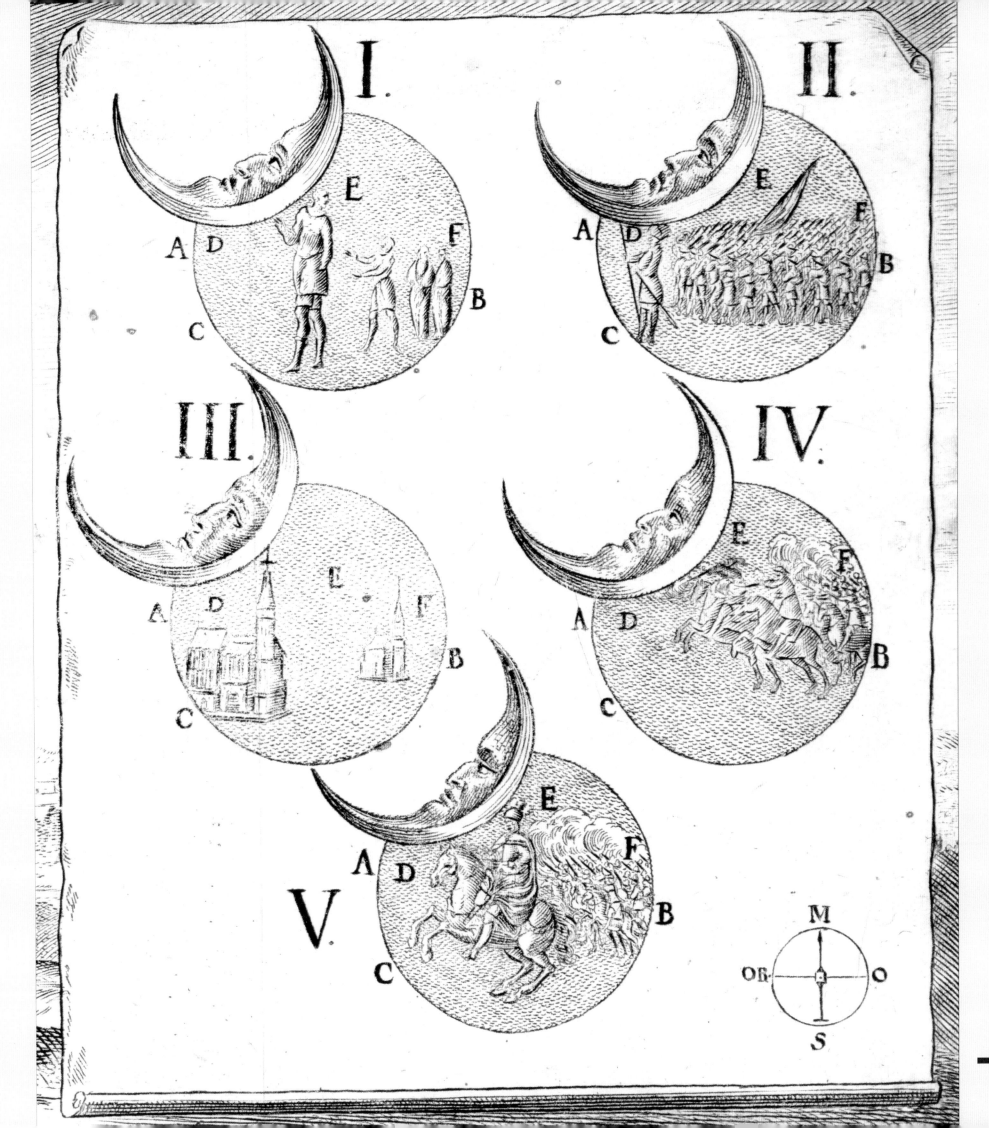

the Seven Wonders of the World, the seven years of famine that Joseph correctly predicted from the Pharaohs' dream, and the seven liberal arts and sciences: Grammar, Rhetoric, Logic, Arithmetic, Music, Astronomy and Geometry.

The Worshipful Master explains that the study

it has allowed him to rise above the level of the brute beasts and make sense of his place in the universe, plot the movement of the planets and predict the cycle of the seasons.

In fact, Geometry is such an essential component of Freemasonry that the two may even be considered as

of this last science is central to the Masonic Order, for Geometry has enabled mankind not only to produce magnificent edifices to help the mind focus on the divine,

synonymous and its laws extend to the very foundation of the Cosmos itself. Hence the Supreme Being is called the Great Architect.

The Steps of Freemasonry
1st Degree - Entered Apprentice
2nd Degree - Fellow Craft
3rd Degree - Master Mason

In recognition of this, a huge golden letter G hangs from the ceiling or adorns the wall behind the Master's chair. The letter is also found on the insignia of Craft Masonry, along with the square and compass.

MASTER MASON

The preparation for the degree of Master Mason is similar to the two prior degrees, in that the initiate is blindfolded, divested of metal objects and a cable-tow is looped around the neck. This time however, his entire chest is bare and both arms are left out of his shirtsleeves.

Assured that the oath he is about to take will not prejudice the service and loyalty he owes to his God, country or family, he is led to the altar where he goes down on both knees. This time he places both hands palm down on the compass and square, which rest on the book of his chosen faith. The legs of the compass lie above the square.

Following the Worshipful Master's lead he repeats the oath.

"I, ____, of my own free will and accord, in the presence of Almighty God, and this worshipful lodge of Master Masons, dedicated to God and the holy Saints John, do hereon most solemnly and sincerely swear, in addition to my former obligations, that I will not reveal the secrets of the Master Mason's degree to anyone of inferior degree, nor to any other being in the known world, except it be to a true and lawful brother or brethren Master Masons, within a body of a just and lawfully constituted lodge of such, and not unto him or them whom I shall only hear to be so, but unto him and them only whom I shall prove to be so, after strict trial and due examination, or lawful information received.

"Furthermore do I promise and swear that I will not give the Master's word, which I shall hereafter receive, neither in the lodge nor out of it, except it be on the five points of fellowship, and then not above my breath.

"Furthermore do I promise and swear that I will not give the Grand Hailing Sign of Distress except I am in real distress, or for the benefit of the Craft when at work, and should I ever see that sign given or the word accompanying it, and the person who gave it appearing to be in distress, I will fly to his relief at the risk of my life, should there be a greater probability of saving his life than losing my own.

"Furthermore do I promise and swear that I will not be at the initiating, passing, or raising of a candidate in a clandestine lodge, I knowing it to be such.

"Furthermore do I promise and swear that I will not be at the initiating of an old man in his dotage, a young man in his nonage, an atheist, an irreligious libertine, an idiot, madman, or woman. Furthermore do I promise and swear that I will not have illegal carnal intercourse with a Master Mason's wife, mother, sister, or daughter, I knowing them to be such, nor suffer it to be done by others, if in my power to prevent it.

"Furthermore do I promise that a Master Mason's secrets, given to me as such, and I knowing them to be such, shall remain as secure and inviolable in my breast as in his own, when communicated to me, murder and treason excepted, and then they left to my own election.

"Furthermore do I promise and swear that I will go on a Master Mason's errand whenever required, even should I have to go barefoot and bare-headed, if within the length of my cable-tow.

"Furthermore do I promise and swear that I will always remember a brother Master Mason when on my knees offering up my devotions to Almighty God.

"Furthermore do I promise and swear that I will aid and assist all poor, indigent Master Masons, their wives and orphans, wheresoever disposed around the globe, as far as is in my power, without materially injuring myself or my family.

"Furthermore do I promise and swear that if any part of my solemn oath of obligation be omitted at this time, I will hold myself amenable thereto whenever informed. To all of which do I most sincerely promise and swear, with a fixed and steady purpose of mind in me to keep and perform the same, binding myself under no less penalty than to have my body severed in twain and divided to the North and South, my bowels burnt to ashes in the center, and the ashes scattered before the four winds of heaven, that there might not be the least track or trace of remembrance remaining among men, or Masons, of so vile and perjured wretch as I should be, were I ever to prove wilfully guilty of violating any part of this my solemn oath and obligation of a Master Mason. So help me God, and keep me steadfast in the due performance of the same."

The oath taken, it is safe to remove the blindfold.

The Master Mason learns the secret signs and passwords of the degree, such as the penal sign, in which the hand, palm down, slashes across the stomach. For the due-guard he assumes the position he took to make the oath, that is to say with both forearms straight out, palms facing the floor and his upper arms close to the sides.

The Master also learns the Grand Hailing Sign of Distress to summon the help of fellow Master Masons when in dire need. For this the upper arms are held straight out and the forearms vertical, with the hands above head height, with the palms facing out. In the dark, when a visual sign would go unheeded, a verbal sign is necessary: "O Lord, my God, is there no help for a Son of a Widow?"

At this point the initiate thinks the ceremony is over and indeed he is led out of the room to get changed into his Master's apron and bedeck himself with the ribbon and jewel of a Senior Deacon. He is therefore taken aback when he returns to the lodge room to hear the Worshipful Master tell him that he will not be a full-fledged Master Mason until he has travelled a road full of peril and danger, meeting with thieves and murderers.

And so he is blindfolded once more and led around the room by the Senior Deacon who relates the story of the murder of Hiram Abiff, the master builder of the Temple of Solomon, identified by the Mason with the biblical figure known as the "son of a widow of Naphtali." He was one of the three Grand Masters of Freemasonry, alongside King Solomon and the King of Tyre, also called Hiram.

Freemasonry has grown since the days of meetings in rooms above taverns and coffee houses as shown from this illustration of a grand dinner in Freemason's Hall, London

Every day at noon during the construction of the Temple, Hiram Abiff would come into the Sanctum Sanctorum, the Holy of Holies, to draw up the plans for the following day's work. This done, he would make his devotions and leave by the south gate of the temple courtyard.

At this point the initiate "becomes" Hiram Abiff as ritual and legend collide. The Conductor guides him to the symbolic south gate and he is suddenly seized by an attacker whom he cannot see. He hears a strange voice demanding to know the secrets of a Master Mason, for the Fellow Crafts had been promised that when the Temple was complete, the secrets would be revealed but they are impatient to travel abroad and receive the honor and reward due a Master Mason.

The Conductor answers on "Hiram's" behalf, reminding the attacker, whose name is Jubela, that the secrets will only be revealed once the Temple is complete and he is found worthy. Jubela threatens murder if his wish is not granted, but Hiram is undaunted so Jubela passes the twenty-four inch gauge across the initiate's throat and the Conductor leads him onto the west gate of the temple.

Here he is attacked by Jubelo who issues the same demands and threats and then strikes "Hiram" on the chest with the square, when he is denied.

At the east gate, Jubelum awaits him and strikes him on the head with his setting-maul, whereon he falls down dead.

Lying on the ground, still blindfolded, "Hiram" hears the three assassins conspiring as to what to do with the body. They decide to bury it until midnight in a pile of rubble and he is wrapped in a blanket and carried to the side of the room to symbolize the burial. A bell then sounds midnight and he is carried to a grave on the brow of a hill "west of Mount Moriah" (the Temple Mount).

The conspirators then mark the spot with a sprig of acacia and make good their escape across the Red Sea towards Ethiopia.

At this point, "Hiram" hears the hubbub of confused voices and then the clear authoritative tones of the Worshipful Master (playing the role of King Solomon) cuts through them, demanding to know the reason for the uproar. He is told that the Grand Master is missing and without him the building of the Temple cannot proceed.

A search is undertaken and once again the initiate hears the sounds of frenetic activity. Unsuccessful, a role-call is taken and the three "Juwes" (Jubelo, Jubela, and Jubelum) are discovered to be absent.

Twelve Fellow Crafts are sent after them, three to the east, three to the west, three to the north and three to the south. More voices reveal that the three from the west have heard reports of the fugitives trying to board a ship out of Joppa (now the port of Jaffa) but then turning back inland towards Jerusalem.

The search for the fugitives goes on for fifteen "days"

without success until one of the Fellow Crafts discovers the sprig of acacia just as another group arrive on the spot to relate that they heard voices saying,

"Oh that my throat had been cut across, my tongue torn out by its roots, and my body buried in the rough sands of the sea at low-water mark, where the tide ebbs and flows twice in twenty-four hours, ere I had been accessory to the death of so good a man as our Grand master, Hiram Abiff."

The second voice, that of Jubelo, answered,

"Oh, that my breast had been torn open, my heart and vitals taken from thence and thrown over my left shoulder, carried into the Valley of Jehosaphat, there to become prey to the wild beasts of the field and the vultures of the air ere I had conspired in the death of so good a man as our Grand Master Hiram Abiff."

The third voice, Jubelum cries,

"Ah, Jubela and Jubelum, it was I that struck him harder than you both! It was I that gave him the fatal blow. It was I that killed him! Oh, that my body had been severed in twain, my bowels taken from thence and burned to ashes, the ashes scattered to the four winds of

Symbolic Meanings:
The Trowel symbolizes "the noble and glorious purpose of spreading the cement of brotherly love and affection".
The Square stands for morality, honesty and fair dealing.
The Compass symbolizes truth and loyalty.
The Bee is a symbol of industry, obedience and rebirth.

heaven, that there might not be the least track or trace of remembrance among men, or Masons, of so vile and perjured wretch as I am."

Returning to the spot where the voices were heard, they capture the fugitives and bring them before King Solomon, who decides that they should meet the fate they called down upon themselves. The initiate then hears the three Juwes being taken out of the room to have their sentences executed, whereupon a voice announces that justice has been done.

King Solomon orders that a search be made for the body of Hiram, in case he left some clue as to how to proceed with the building of the Temple.

At the spot where the acacia had been so easily uprooted, the twelve Fellow Crafts find the initiate, and pull him from his blanket "grave". The smell of decomposition overwhelms them and they put out their hands in the palm down position of the due-guard to protect themselves.

On his body, they find only the ribbon and jewel of the Senior Deacon, which was given to him when he thought the ceremony completed. Thus it appears that the Master's word is lost forever.

Solomon now turns to the King of Tyre, played by the Lodge Treasurer. He ordains that the first word spoken and the first sign given at the grave shall stand in for "That-Which-Was-Lost" until it is found at some point in the future and can once again be used in the rule of the Master Mason's degree.

The initiate is surrounded in his grave. Solomon gives the Grand Hailing Sign of Distress, with both palms facing forward, and cries, "Oh, Lord is there no help for the Widow's Son?"

He then calls for the body to be raised from its temporary grave and the grip of an Entered Apprentice tries to lift it. The grip is not strong enough however and the flesh starts to slip from the body, such is the state of decomposition. Next the grip of the Fellow Craft is tried

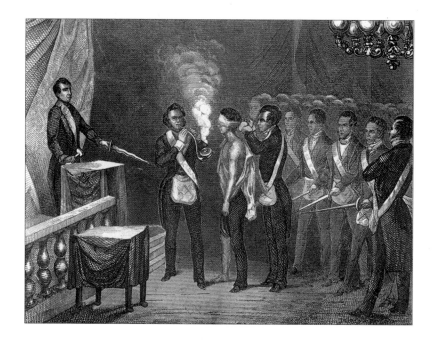

but once again it is not equal to the job. Finally, Solomon himself steps up to the grave and uses the grip of the Master Mason, known as the "Lion's Paw" to raise "Hiram" from his prone position on the floor.

The initiate is then placed in the "five points of fellowship", with his right foot inside the right foot of the Worshipful Master, their right knees together, their left hands on one another's back, and their mouths up against each other's ear, as you would if you wanted to whisper a secret.

The basis of the five points is then explained;

Initiation of a Master Mason.

Foot-to-Foot, because of a Master Mason will go out of his way to assist his brothers.

Knee-to-Knee, because a Master Mason will always pray for a brother before he prays for himself.

Breast-to-Breast, because a Master Mason will keep the secrets of his brother closer to his heart than he would his own.

The blindfold now removed, the candidate is told that Hiram's body was taken and buried with much reverence beneath the Holy of Holies of the Temple, where the Ark of the Covenant would be placed. Hence the designation of the Master Mason's Lodge as the Sanctum Sanctorum. To commemorate his life, a monument was built of a beautiful virgin, with a sprig of

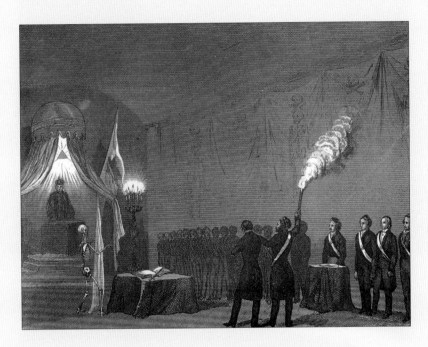

Hand-to-Back, because a Master Mason will watch his brother's back, and defend his reputation, when he is not there to defend it himself.

Mouth-to-Ear, because a Master Mason will always seek to give his brother the best advice, so that one unknowingly leaving the path of wisdom can be recalled before it is too late.

Sometimes, the Master's word "Mahabone" is whispered to the initiate, and then whispered back. He is warned only to repeat the word in the "five points of fellowship" configuration.

acacia in her right hand and an urn in her left. Before her was a broken column and an open book. Behind her stood Father Time, counting the ringlets in her hair. The book was the eternal record of the achievements of the Grand Master, the broken column the unfinished Temple and work of Hiram Abiff. The sprig of acacia symbolized his immortality, in spite of his mortal nature symbolized by the ashes in his urn. And finally the figure of Father Time is a reminder that anything is possible through patience and perseverance.

33rd Degree Initiation.

A funeral procession.

These are the essentials of the rituals of the three degrees of Craft Masonry, which is the original and most prevalent form of Freemasonry, however there are higher degrees in some forms of Freemasonry, most notably the Ancient and Accepted Rite, which has thirty-three degrees in total, although one Masonic historian claims to have identified fourteen hundred degrees!

After Entered Apprentice, Fellow Craft and Master Mason it ascends as follows:

Ancient Regalia

4   Secret Master
5   Perfect Master
6   Intimate Secretary
7   Provost and Judge
8   Intendant of the Building
9   Elect of Nine
10 Elect of Fifteen
11 Sublime effect
12 Grand Master Architect
13 Royal Arch (of Enoch)
14 Scottish Knight of Perfection
15 Knight of the Sword, or of the East
16 Prince of Jerusalem
17 Knight of the East and West
18 Knight of the Pelican and Eagle and
    Sovereign Prince Rose Croix of Heredom
19 Grand Pontiff
20 Venerable Grand Master
21 Patriarch Noachite
22 Prince of Libanus
23 Chief of the Tabernacle
24 Prince of the Tabernacle
25 Knight of the Brazen Serpent
26 Prince of Mercy
27 Commander of the Temple
28 Knight of the Sun
29 Knight of St. Andrew
30 Grand Elected Knight Kadosh, Knight
    of the Black and White Eagle
31 Grand Inspector Inquisitor Commander
32 Sublime Prince of the Royal Secret
33 Grand Inspector General

According to Stephen Knight, before his book "The Brotherhood" came out in 1984, most Master Masons would have thought they had achieved the highest rank in Freemasonry and would have been entirely unaware of the thirty degrees above them. Freemasons who had attained these higher ranks would no longer be subject to a provincial or national Grand Lodge but to a Supreme Council, the most senior being the Supreme Council of Charleston, USA. He concludes that these are among the most powerful men in the world.

However, the practice of awarding side degrees goes back to the eighteenth century. To be awarded to the Royal Arch degree in America one had to be a Master Mason of good standing. They were organized under chapters rather than lodges and the first among them conferred four degrees known as the Capitular Rite: Mark Master, Past Master (Virtual), Most Excellent Master and the Royal Arch.

There is also the Templar Rite, only open to a Royal Arch Mason of good standing. Known as the Grand Encampment of Knights Templar of the United States of America they have three orders: Red Cross, Knights of Malta and Knights Templar. The main point of difference to Craft Masonry is that members must be Christian whereas Craft Masonry only refuses entry to atheists.

The sword is a Masonic emblem of truth and justice

  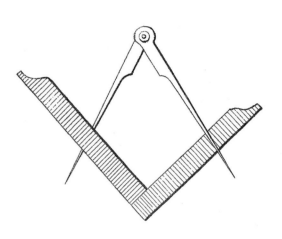

chapter 3

MUCH HAS BEEN MADE OF THE POSSIBILITY THAT THE ORIGINS OF FREEMASONRY LIE IN THE MEDIEVAL ORDER CALLED THE POOR FELLOW-SOLDIERS OF CHRIST AND THE TEMPLE OF SOLOMON ALSO KNOWN BY ITS MORE POPULAR NAME THE KNIGHTS TEMPLAR. SO LET US NOW EXAMINE THIS ORDER OF WARRIOR MONKS WHICH HAS EXERTED SUCH A ROMANTIC INFLUENCE ON THE POPULAR IMAGINATION.

The Order of Knights Templar was an important force in medieval Europe. According to Masonic traditions, Scottish Freemasonry was founded by some Knights who may have escaped to Scotland.

The Templar

In June 1099 after a gruelling journey in which they had been beset every step of the way not only by enemy ambush but by the extremes of weather and the privations of an army on the march, the Crusaders finally arrived before the walls of Jerusalem and found that their troubles were only just beginning. The wells outside the city had been poisoned on the orders of the Egyptian governor, and the peasants' flocks driven away. There was no shade from the searing heat of the sun and this was not just insufferable for men in full battle dress, it also meant there was no local timber to build the machines of war necessary to take a walled city.

There were already plenty of Christians living in Jerusalem, who were well tolerated by the Moslems but the governor thought that by expelling them he would transfer the burden of feeding them onto the Crusaders.

As it turned out, this was a fatal error for among them was a man named Gerard, master of the Amalfi hostelry for Christian pilgrims and he had a great deal of information to share on the weak points of the fortifications.

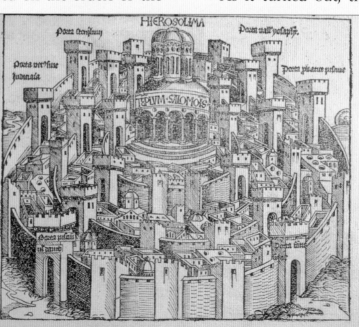

A medieval illustration of Jerusalem with the Temple of Solomon shown at the top

Jerusalem fell after a siege that lasted nine days, and there followed scenes of the most shameful carnage as the triumphant invaders inflicted a frenzied vengeance on the enemy that is hinted at in a report sent to the pope:

"If you would hear how we treated our enemies in Jerusalem, know that in the portico of Solomon and in the Temple our men rode through the unclean blood of the Saracens, which came up to the knees of their horses."

For his part in the victory, the monks who ran the Amalfi hostelry were given grants of land and gifts of treasure and with Jerusalem opened up they grew into a

Pledging themselves to a life of poverty, chastity and obedience their raison d'etre would be the protection of pilgrims. Little is known of the actions of the new order over the next nine years, except that it seems they took in no new members and were quartered in a wing of the royal palace, the former al—Aqsa mosque, which stood on the site of the Temple of Solomon.

Then in 1127, Pope Honarius was petitioned on behalf of the Templars by the abbot of Clairvaux, Saint Bernard, who was a man of such prestige in the church that he was known as the "second pope". A council was convened at Troyes where the order was granted official papal recognition and a Rule was established, governing the daily lives and activities of the Templars.

Connection

large and thriving order. In 1118 they decided to expand their operation to include knights who would devote themselves to protecting the Christian pilgrims, pouring in from all over Europe. They changed their name to the Hospital of Saint John of Jerusalem and would ever after be known as the Hospitallers.

Prompted no doubt by the success of this order, Hugh de Payans, a vassal of the Count of Champagne, petitioned King Baldwin II for royal sanction of an order he intended to establish with eight other knights.

The council of Troyes marked a changing point in the fortunes of the order. With papal sanction, the Templars transcended all sovereign authority and were answerable only to the pope. Laying down their lives in the defense of Christians making the pilgrimage to the Holy Land was seen as such a worthy and honorable cause that gifts and new recruits flooded in, especially from Europe's noble families. Service in the Templars was said to be sufficient penance to expiate the guilt of any crime, even the worst of all, heresy.

This was to prove significant in the years to come when the Church would seek to suppress the order, on the grounds of desecrating the cross and the holy sacrament. It is quite probable that during the Albigensian crusade, when the Cathar heretics in southern France were massacred, a number of the high-ranking Cathar nobles may have joined the order. No doubt the presence of such freethinkers would have opened the Templar minds to the various Gnostic and Dualist heresies that had gone underground to escape persecution by the Church.

The order grew rich very rapidly. For a start, the vow of chastity precluded the ownership of property, which meant everything from property and land, right down to the smallest of pocket books. It all had to be donated to the order upon entry as was any loot taken in battle and if a Templar knight was captured on the field,

Religious artwork was predominant during the Middle Ages

he could not be ransomed. However, it usually never got to this stage, as the knights could not retreat unless the odds against them were at least three to one. Even in the face of overwhelming odds, a commander might order his men to fight to the death and they would have to obey.

Over the next two centuries, some 20,000 initiates were to join the order, the vast majority of them from the nobility. Second-born sons might bring a dowry of money with them, first-borns their entire inheritance. It was reckoned at the time that the Templars owned over nine thousand revenue-producing manors, as well as mills and markets. Add to this the donations from the Church in Rome and revenue earned from transporting crusaders and pilgrims to the Holy Land in Templar-owned ships and it will be appreciated what an immensely wealthy order the Templars were. But this is not even the whole story.

As servants of God who had pledged themselves to an extremely austere and dangerous life, the Templars were viewed as one of the most trustworthy institutions in Europe. They already had the means and the manpower to guard their immense fortune, it was not long before noble families across Europe realized that here was one of the most reliable safe deposits for their wealth when they travelled abroad. In fact, so secure were their vaults and such trust placed in their honesty that the crown jewels of the English royal family were placed with them for a time.

Richard Coeur de Lion, overseeing the execution of the Saracens

It was not long before they expanded from safety deposit to the issuing of paper for money, maintaining trusts for noble scions and even a precursor of mortgage banking. The issuance of paper money is something we take for granted nowadays but would have been incredibly useful to someone wanting to transfer funds overseas. The only alternative available at the time was to physically transport the gold and silver there yourself, which was a risky venture.

If the system is to escape outside exploitation however, it requires a very effective network of communication, with means of verifying identification. With the military network that was already in place, this would not have proved too big a step. From their dealings with the Saracens, the Templars were well-versed in the cut-and-thrust of espionage and counter-espionage, and the practice of using codes to conceal operations intelligence was already highly evolved.

Secret agents, many of them Moslems, were on the Templar payroll in cities all along the coast of the Mediterranean in both continents. Their influence extended even to Cairo, where they employed the emir al-Fakhri as a double agent.

The necessarily clandestine nature of much of the Templar activity added to the air of mystery that shrouded the organization. But it was not just those on the outside looking in who were kept in the dark, the atmosphere of secrecy

Richard Coeur de Lion departing the Holy Land

Templars, serving mass and hearing confession. They dressed in a green mantle with a red cross and always wore gloves to keep their hands clean for "when they touch God." Because the knights were illiterate they also acted as scribes. In contrast to the knights, they were clean-shaven.

Right at the top of the order was the Grandmaster, who ruled the order with absolute authority. His headquarters were in Jerusalem and as well as holding the position of abbot he was a full-equipped and trained knight, who expected to die on the battlefield. Of twenty-one grandmasters in total, ten died in action.

Strict secrecy was observed between the classes and between the different ranks within each class. Knowledge of the Rule would be gradually revealed as an initiate rose through the ranks. Only those at the very top of the hierarchy would be in full possession of the Templar secrets. Such importance was placed on hermetically sealing each rung of the order, that meetings could only take place with guards outside with drawn swords and any breach of the oath of secrecy resulted in expulsion from the order and in some cases even death.

Thus the Templars' reputation for secrecy was well-deserved and when the order was brutally suppressed in 1307, it played a crucial role in the fate of those who managed to survive the initial wave of persecution.

The fortunes of the Christian powers in the Holy Land waxed and waned in the two centuries following the formation of the Templars but in 1291 the last Christian stronghold at Acre fell to the Mamelukes, and

pervaded the internal infrastructure of the order.

There were three classes: the knights, the sergeants and the clerics.

Those in the knightly class were designated full brothers and they were required not just to be "free", that is to say not born as a bondsman or serf, but also to derive from the nobility. They wore a white mantle with a red eight-pointed cross and a sheepskin girdle which symbolized their oath of chastity. They wore their hair very short but did not cut their beards.

The Sergeants were recruited from the free bourgeoisie. They wore a black mantle with a red cross and performed the duties of squires and sentries.

The clerics attended to the pastoral care of the

with it went a significant portion of the Templar wealth and possessions.

They set up base on the island of Cyprus, but ran into trouble because of the threat such a well-equipped and well-trained standing army posed to the sovereign King Henry. Compounding this issue for an order, which recognized no authority save the pope, was the problem of what to do now that their whole raison d'etre of providing safe passage to the Holy Land for Christian pilgrims, was redundant.

They were eager for another crusade, but the response from the Church and the ruling families of Europe was not favorable.

In 1306 Pope Clement V called the Grandmaster of the Templars to Poitiers to discuss the possibility of a new crusade. The Teutonic Knights were attempting to conquer the pagans in north-eastern Europe and the Hospitallers were busy trying to establish a base on Rhodes, which they finally managed in 1308 and from then on were known as the Knights of Rhodes.

Little did they know it then but the days of the Templars were numbered and powerful men were plotting their downfall and the division of the spoils. King Philip IV of France had long looked on the Templar wealth with greedy eyes. He had borrowed heavily from the Templar treasury to finance his wars against King Edward I of England. To strike at the Templars would be a double-blow, at once cancelling the debt and plundering their legendary wealth.

He had a long history of problems with the papacy, so much so that at one point he actually arranged for the

kidnap of Boniface VIII who was so badly treated he died soon afterwards. He finally got a compliant pope in the shape of Bernard de Goth, archbishop of Bordeaux, who was to become Clement V in 1305. In return for rigging the election, Bernard de Goth is said to have agreed to play his part in the suppression of the Templars but Philip IV would not just accept an oath to that effect, he took two of his brothers and two nephews as hostages.

Philip IV had many reasons to be grateful to the Templars, for aside from loaning him the dowry for his daughter to wed King Edward II of England, they had sheltered him in their Paris temple when the mob rioted for three days. Despite the debt of gratitude he owed, his intention was to hijack a plan, which the pope had been

Jacques de Molay, Grand Master
of the Knights Templar

discussing of merging the Templars and the Hospitallers into a single order called "The Knights of Jerusalem" under the leadership of the Hospitaller Grandmaster, Foulques de Villaret. Philip's idea was to lead the orders himself under the title "Rex Bellator" or "War King" and hence gain control of the wealth of the combined orders but with no backers he settled for the wealth of the Templars. With the death of Edward I and the succession of his weak son, Edward II, he would be able at last to wage a campaign against the English territories in France.

His chief spymaster Philip de Nogaret arranged for sealed orders to be sent all over France, with the strict instructions not to be opened until the morning of Friday 13 October 1307 just in case the Templars had infiltrated his network of secret agents. De Nogaret had been responsible for the simultaneous arrest of every Jew in France and their mass expulsion without their possessions or property the year before and was very capable of masterminding an operation that relied on the utmost secrecy for its success.

Meanwhile a campaign of propaganda spread rumors of blasphemy and sodomy amongst the Templar orders, which appeared to be confirmed when a Templar Knight who had been expelled, "confessed" to spitting and trampling on the cross and worshipping a bearded deity called Baphomet.

Jacques de Molay was blissfully unaware of his impending doom as he was accorded the highest honor by King Philip IV who asked him to act as pallbearer for the body of his sister-in-law, Princess Catherine of Valois.

The next day as the seneschals of France moved to seize the fifteen thousand Templars in France, the pulpits rang with the charges of heresy and sodomy designed to whip up moral outrage against the order which had hitherto enjoyed popular support. With the Templars in chains the Dominican Grand Inquisitor went to work on them exacting confessions of blasphemy with torture.

On November 22, the bull Pastoralis Preeminentae went out from Pope Clement V to all Christian monarchs calling for the Europe-wide arrest and torture of all Templars.

As members of a holy order they should have been

exempt from torture, and they must have been utterly dismayed that the only temporal authority to which they were subject, the Holy Mother Church, was now ordering that no "known means of torture" should be spared in the investigation of their crimes.

So enthusiastic was the Inquisition that 36 Templars died within the first few days of their arrest. The scale of the operation was such that there were simply not enough traditional instruments of torture, such as the rack and the wheel, to go around, so the method most commonly used was to apply red hot pincers to the skin or to douse the feet in oil and roast them slowly over a fire. As members of another holy order, the Inquisitors were forbidden to spill blood, but they got round this imposition with a mixture of imagination and enthusiasm for the work in hand and there were many ingeniously sickening devices for inflicting pain without breaking the skin.

Under such duress it is readily understandable that many Templars confessed to the trumped up charges against them, among which were allegations that they had collaborated with the Moslems to drive the Christians out of the Holy Land. The main drive of the Inquisitors however was to extract confessions of heresy, punishable by the confiscation of property, which was King Philip

IV's objective from the beginning. And under the law of the day, once a confession had been made it was deemed irrevocable, even though we realize nowadays that a man will say anything his interrogators want to hear just to stop the pain. Worst of all for the Templars, if they subsequently denied the heresy which they had admitted under torture, they were deemed a "relapsed heretic" and the only possible punishment for this was to be burnt at the stake.

Outside France the Templars fared somewhat better. In Germany the Templar preceptor Hugo of Gumbach, accompanied by twenty knights in full battle armor, stormed into the council of the archbishop of Metz declaring himself ready to answer to the vile charges of the pope in the ordeal of trial by combat. Unsurprisingly, no one was ready to take him up on the offer.

In Spain and Portugal, the Templars were too important in the war against the Moslem occupiers to throw away their help so lightly and they were found innocent, so much so that in Portugal their allegiance was transferred from the pope to the king and in recognition of their honorable conduct they were renamed the Knights of Christ.

On April 13th 1312, the Templars were finally disbanded as an order, even though the pope had balked

The island of Cyprus would become the central base
for the Templar Order and remained the home of Grand Master
Jacques de Molay until his imprisonment in 1307

vō · Lüttishofen ·

of formally condemning as heretical an order which was beholden unto him alone. So no charges were ever found against the Templars despite the wealth of "evidence" which the Dominican Inquisitors of the Congregation of the Holy Office had found against it.

In May another bull, Ad Providum, decreed that the entire property of the Templars be transferred to the Hospitallers. Philip IV had to content himself with recouping from that property the expenses incurred for the arrest, torture and imprisonment of the Templars in the four years since their downfall.

Members of the lower ranks who had confessed were allowed to go free, though many of them were broken men. The highest-ranking Templars, including Jacques de Molay, the Grandmaster, were to publicly confess their guilt on a platform especially erected outside the Notre Dame Cathedral in Paris.

As he mounted the steps he must have known that to retract at this late hour and embarrass the Church would mean an agonizing death, and he was a frail old man over seventy years old, who had by now spent over six years in prison. And yet he summoned up the courage to martyr himself when a lesser man would have taken the offer of a pension and somewhere out of the way to spend his remaining years.

"I think it only right," he said, when the crowd fell silent, "that at so solemn a moment when my life has so little time to run I should reveal the deception which has been practiced and speak up for the truth. Before heaven and earth and all of you here as my witnesses, I admit that I am guilty of the grossest iniquity. But the iniquity is that I have lied in admitting the disgusting charges laid against the order. I declare, and I must declare, that the order is innocent. Its purity and saintliness are beyond question. I have indeed confessed that the order is guilty, but I have done so only to save myself from terrible tortures by saying what my enemies wished me to say. Other knights who have retracted their confessions have been led to the stake, yet the thought of dying is not so awful that I shall confess to foul crimes, which have never been committed. Life is offered to me, but at the price of infamy. At such a price, life is not worth living. I do not grieve that I must die if life can be bought only by piling one lie upon another."

As he no doubt knew, the revenge of the Church and Crown would be swift and cruel. Even as he was bundled off stage, the announcement of his death went out that he would burn for his sins that very evening. He must have known that every effort would be made to ensure his passing from this world would be as painful as possible. At public hangings, the executioner could be paid in advance to hang his weight upon the body and thus cause a quick painless death from a broken neck. Likewise with

In 1811 Mohammed Ali massacred the Mamelukes, and became viceroy of Egypt

burning at the stake, the fire could be stoked so that the intense heat consumed the victim very quickly or green boughs could be added to produce smoke which would cause death by smoke inhalation. Potions could be given to render the victim senseless by the time the flames were licking about his body.

But for de Molay, a pyre of dry wood and charcoal would ensure that he was conscious throughout as he was slowly roasted and the pain would be as much as any one man had ever experienced.

As he burned, he cursed King Philip and his family for thirteen generations to come and called for the king and pope to meet him within the year to answer for their crimes before the throne of God. Clement V was dead before a month was out and Philip died before the end of the year. Legend has it that at the execution of King Louis XVI in the French Revolution, an unidentified man leapt onto the scaffold and began flicking the blood spilt from his severed neck into the crowd, shouting "Jacques de Molay, thou art revenged!"

Meanwhile in England, the Templars had fared rather better than their continental brothers. The weak and ineffectual Prince of Wales had succeeded to the throne three months before the arrest of the Templars in France. Had he been a stronger ruler, he would still have been unwilling to move against the Templars, for the relationship between the Crown and the order was a good one. It was in the grounds of the London Temple, that many of the noble peers of the young Prince spent the night before being knighted at Westminster in preparation for the oncoming war against Robert the Bruce and many Templars had laid down their lives in the service of his father, Edward I, the most notable being Brian de Jay, Master of the English Temple.

His indecision provided the English Templars with a vital window to make good their plans for escape for it was not long before word arrived of the dreadful fate of their brothers on the continent.

It was not until December 15 that the King received the papal bull Pastoralis Preeminentae, promulgated on November 22, which forced his hand. But even then, the orders calling for their arrest did not go out until January 7 and from their announcement in London they took a while to reach the rest of the country.

Even in France, despite the utmost secrecy behind the simultaneous arrests, some Templars managed to escape. We know for a fact that none of the eighteen Templar-owned ships in the port of La Rochelle were ever captured and much of the wealth in the Templar treasury, which was so coveted by Philip IV, had also disappeared.

The English Templars had two months between the arrests in France and the arrival of the papal bull in which to plan their escape. Consequently when soldiers arrived at the Temple in London, there was no one of significant

An audience with Pope Honorius III

rank to arrest, all the records had been destroyed and the famed Templar wealth was gone. In all England only two fugitive Templars were taken. Those who had chosen to stay and face their accusers were treated civilly, permitted to remain under house arrest.

The Inquisition had no authority in England, and although they were allowed to interview the prisoners they were not permitted to torture them, a situation which infuriated the pope. Such was his fanatic zeal on the matter that he despatched ten professional torturers from the continent, with words threatening Edward I with excommunication if he did not comply with papal authority. And so, at the instigation of the Church in Rome, the use of torture was permitted for the first time in English jurisprudence.

Perhaps because of the restraint urged by Edward I in the treatment of the Templar prisoners or the fact that they had been incarcerated for two years by then and their resolve was strengthened, no confessions of heresy were extracted. There were many break-outs from prison, which points to collusion and not a single escapee was recaptured, which points to sympathy or at least apathy in the matter of their apprehension.

Needless to say as soon as the use of torture was instituted in the interrogation of the Templars in England, the stakes became very high for those men on the run.

Joseph of Arimathea

They were lucky in one respect however. Across the border in Scotland, Robert the Bruce was preparing for war with England. Vastly outnumbered, with a bedraggled yet courageous army, many armed only with farm tools, he was not going to arrest and torture any knights fleeing persecution from the English. With the motto "the enemy of my enemy is my friend" he ignored the papal bull of Pope Clement V and Scotland became a safe haven for the fugitive Templars.

According to legend, a group of Templar knights fought alongside Robert the Bruce at the famous Battle of Bannockburn forming part of the unit of armored cavalry whose role was to break up the ranks of English longbowmen, so deadly on the field.

This is not however to say that the Templars could declare themselves with impunity once they had crossed the border. The religious orders in Scotland would certainly have done their best to see the instructions of the pope carried out.

And so the Templars vanish from the annals of history. It would be difficult to imagine that they would simply disappear altogether. If nothing else, the desire to avenge their betrayal would have been enough to keep the order alive. It must also be borne in mind that if any order had the means to survive underground it was the Templars. For a start there was the famed Templar wealth,

which was spirited away before the usurpers could get their hands on it.

A man on the run needs a safe place to stay, a contact in the next town, a means of recognizing and being recognized by that contact, and the directions and wherewithal to get to the next port of call. The Templars had a two hundred-year history of dealing with espionage and counter espionage, with the use of passwords and the means of verifying identification.

Under the weak and ineffectual rule of Edward I, the country was in a very unstable state. Authority was decentralized and lay in the hands of the lords ordainers, who looked to their own personal gain.

This was the era of Robin Hood, when bands of outlaws and robber barons preyed on the conspicuous and ill-gotten wealth of the Church. In fact it is not unreasonable to assume that some of the legends built around noble and virtuous outlaws living in the forests of northern England and redistributing the wealth of the common people may have been based on stories of fugitive Templars.

As we examine the problems that a fugitive Templar might face when on the run we begin perhaps to see the origins of what may have become the rituals of the secret society that declared itself in 1717 as the Freemasons.

It is perhaps no coincidence that many Freemasons regard Scottish Craft Freemasonry as the original and purest form.

Heading north across the English countryside would have been fraught with danger. For a start nearly a third

One of the great temples of the ancient Egyptians, was the Grand Temple on the island of Philae. The Egyptians worshipped the sun and the sun god. Freemasons seek the inner light and spiritual enlightenment.

of the land was owned by the Church. There was also the problem of the laws on vagrancy. An itinerant stranger was not just looked upon with suspicion and curiosity, he could be locked up in the town jail, if he did not have a

'Historiated letters' embellish a story or convey further meaning about a passage.
'Inhabited letters' contain images of men and beasts.

witness to vouch for his identity. This was an age, which gives us the word "villain", deriving from the "vill", where a tenant farmer was forced to reside, in a state of near bondage to the lord of the manor.

This may well explain the peculiar stipulation in the Old Charges of Freemasonry that a visiting brother may not go into town unless he has a brother to witness for him.

As to the problem of locating the contact in a new town, one could not simply identify oneself to the first person one saw and ask for directions. Despite the prevailing lawlessness there would have been rewards and people on the lookout for strangers. Perhaps this is the origin of the due-guards. The varying configurations of the hands and arms can be posed very quickly and dismantled almost instantaneously, and if you did not know what to look for you would not realize that a signal had been given. Also the use of the palms can be seen from a long way off, perhaps from far enough to hurry away if one was afraid of having aroused suspicion.

Even the Grand Hailing Sign of Distress "Is there no help for a widow's son?" could be mistaken for the world-weary sigh of a distressed and brow-beaten man. And the exchange, "Are you a traveling man?" "Yes I am." "Where are you traveling?" "From west to east", is the kind of innocuous yet precise covert system of identification that is used by secret agents and underground movements to this day.

Fugitive Templars were not just entrusting their lives to the efficacy and reliability of this network. They knew they would not get a quick death if caught. Rather they would be subject to the most brutal treatment at the hands of the Inquisition who were experts in the art of inflicting as much physical pain as was humanly possible without causing actual death.

For this reason a guarantee was needed, a personal investment in the risk that the fugitive was running. This may be the origin of the controversial oath that a Mason swears on entering each of the three degrees of Craft Masonry.

Each oath details the kind of agonizing death that a Templar himself may have faced if apprehended, asking for a similar fate to be called down on the oath taker should he reveal the secrets of Freemasonry. For a fugitive Templar, to have his secrets revealed meant capture and torture, with death the only thing to look forward to.

Perhaps this is another reason why the Freemasons demand that an initiate believe in a deity. For an atheist, the swearing of oaths is meaningless as there is no corresponding expectation of punishment for breaking it.

For an underground network to survive without fear of exposure there must not only be absolute trust between its members, all possible sources of friction must be eliminated. Once again the question of worship presents itself when we recall to mind the lack of directives on how a brother worships his deity or indeed which deity he worships. When we think of the amount of blood that has been spilled in wars between factions of Christianity, let alone between Christianity and other faiths, we see what a sensible precaution this may have been, if the hypothesis holds true.

The same thinking may explain the oath in which a brother Mason swears that he "will not have illegal carnal intercourse with a Master Mason's wife, mother, sister, or daughter." For such a betrayal of trust may well have led the cuckolded man in a fit of anger to reveal the true identity of the man he has been harboring in his house.

Another apparently inscrutable tent of Freemasonry becomes understandable if we look for the roots in the Templar fugitives. An initiate to the level of Master Mason is told that the degree will make him "a brother to pirates and corsairs." Recalling the eighteen ships that disappeared prior to the arrest of the Templars in France, and the living they may have had to make from plunder on the high seas, could shed light on this mysterious statement.

Tantalizingly there is even a legend that in 1813 the merchant ship Oak captained by a Freemason was boarded by a gang of pirates. As the last act of a desperate man on the point of death, he gave the Grand Hailing Sign of

Entrance to the Holy Sepulcher, Jerusalem

Distress, which was recognized by the pirate, also a Master Mason, who immediately called off his men, apologized and sent the captain on his way.

Another similarity between the Templars and Freemasonry is the pyramidal structure of knowledge, with only those in the upper echelons knowing the whole body of Masonic lore in Freemasonry and only those knights of the first rank of the Templars knowing all the secrets of the Rule. Much stress is placed in the initiation of a Mason through each degree on not divulging the secrets to the uninitiated, and this refers both to those outside the Lodge, and those lower down in the hierarchy.

This is common practice with most secret societies, for it means that if they are infiltrated, the society is broken up only from that level down and with the head still in place will be able to continue to function. Where lives are at stake, the body count will be necessarily restricted.

Some excellent research into the possibility of the roots of Freemasonry lying in the religious order of the Templars has been done by John J. Robinson in his book "Born in Blood. The Lost Secrets of Freemasonry." He examines the mysterious vocabulary that makes up much of the ritual that is so important to Freemasonry. Many writers have tried with little success to link these words to medieval guilds of stone masons but none has provided any satisfactory answers.

With the basic premise that the words have their origins in the medieval French spoken by the chivalric order he has made some intriguing discoveries.

For instance, he has given a convincing derivation of the word "tyler" which is the title of the sergeant-at-arms who stands on guard outside the lodge to make sure that none enter unless they are of the appropriate degree. His role is similar to that of the two knights who guarded the meetings of the high-ranking Templars to prevent the secrets of the Rule being discovered. According to some sources they took their job so seriously that several eavesdroppers were beheaded the moment they were caught.

The French derivation of the word is apparent in its use as "taille" or "cut" which has given us "tailor" and for a man armed with a sword it would be an appropriate appellation.

Similarly the word "due-guard" whose derivation is unclear when searching for an English root, makes more sense when viewed from a French angle. For we have the term "geste du garde" meaning a protective gesture, which has been truncated and anglicized.

More convincingly still he traces the derivation of the "Free" affix of Freemason from the term of address used by members of a religious order such as the Templars. The French for "brother" is "frere", which over time might have become "free".

Intriguing stuff but research such as this can only ever be conjecture. The mysterious beginnings of Freemasonry will remain forever shrouded in secrecy, and we can only

At the Heart of Jerusalem is the Noble Sanctuary, Al-Haram al-Sharif, enclosing over 35 acres of fountains, gardens, buildings and domes. At its southern most end is Al-Aqsa Mosque and at its center the celebrated Dome of the Rock.

guess at the reasons, although some kind of persecution by the Church or Crown or both is highly probable.

The idea of a lodge being a safe place where a fugitive Templar can find rest and refreshment and directions to the next point of contact might explain the stage in the ritual of the first degree in which the candidate is stripped of all metal objects and then reminded that should he ever come across a brother in so destitute a condition he must remember how he was helped by his brother Masons. Such a condition is far more likely to apply to a fugitive from the law than a traveling stone mason.

Thus the original lodges may not have been meeting-places but hiding places,

perhaps a hayloft in a barn or a cellar safe from sight. Before Freemasonry went public in 1717, there would have been no permanent lodge rooms, no Freemasons' halls. Meetings might have been held in the dining-room of taverns and the symbols used would have been portable. The use of cloths painted with the allegorical symbols of speculative Freemasonry is still evident in the aprons that Masons wear during their ceremonies.

Originally, the secret lore of Freemasonry would have been imparted in lecture form and cloths spread out to cover the floor would have been easily rolled out and then put away in a portable form. As Freemasonry became established, the allegorical symbols could be represented in statuary and sculpture and painted on the walls and the ritual of initiation became the preferred teaching medium.

If the hypothesis is correct that the Freemasons derive from Templars fleeing persecution by the Church in medieval England, the original lodge meetings may have taken place in a remote spot in the woods, with the tyler on the lookout for passers-by.

The use of the circle with the point at the center in Masonic ritual may also derive from the circular churches favored by the Templars, deliberately modelled on the

Few could withstand the agonies of the rack of the Spanish Inquisition

Church of the Holy Sepulcher in Jerusalem. Indeed the Templar church in London has a circular stone bench so that the knights could gather together in much the same way as King Arthur's court at Camelot.

If the Templar knights were forced to draw a crude circle in the ground the compass would have assumed a significant place in the ritual as indeed it does in Freemasonry and there would have been a spot left in the centre of the circle which Freemasons equate with the divine source of the Deity.

Similarly the black and white flooring in Masonic lodges may originate in the Templar standard carried into battle, the "Beau Seant" which was black and white, the black symbolizing the world of sin the initiate was leaving behind on joining the order and the white block symbolizing the state of grace he was now entering upon taking his vows before God.

The apron which Freemasons wear was originally an untrimmed white lambskin tied around the waist, supposed to symbolize innocence and purity. This is reminiscent of the Templars, because they had to wear a lambskin girdle at all times as an emblem of chastity.

But perhaps the most significant connection between the Templars and the Freemasons lies in the importance both orders place in the Temple of King Solomon.

As we have seen, the order took its name from the Temple which was supposed to lie beneath the former Al-Aqsa mosque where the Templars made their first headquarters when the order was founded in 1118.

Freemasonry uses the Temple of Solomon as an allegorical symbol to represent the work that a Mason undertakes to perfect himself. For the Masons each man is an unfinished temple in that he requires much hard psychological work to connect to the divine source that is within him. In another sense humanity itself and the progress of mankind is viewed as a Temple, and it is the responsibility of every man to take his rightful place therein, so that the Temple can one day be complete. In this instance the Temple become a means of glorifying God.

The three most important symbols used in the Masonic ritual, known as the three Great Lights, are the volume of sacred law, the compass and the square. They are so central to Masonic lore that no lodge can work unless they are displayed. As a Mason progresses through the three degrees the compass and square are arranged one on top of the other in differing configurations but the basic triangular shape endures of a V over an inverted V. This may be symbologically linked to the reference made to

Robert the Bruce at Bannockburn, Scotland

Masonic meetings "on high hills and in deep valleys" as the tip of the V is reminiscent of a peak and the inverted V forms a trough. Readers interested in the symbology used by Dan Brown in his "The Da Vinci Code" will of course remember the reference to the same symbol used to denote the masculine and feminine principles.

What is even more compelling is the convincing assertion made by John J. Robinson that the compass resting on the square is very similar to the Seal of Solomon, which is identical to the six-sided star of David, except that one of the triangles is outlined and the other solid. The legs of the triangle interlock in a similar way in which the compass and square are positioned for the degree of a Fellow Craft Mason.

Crucially, the Freemasons' legend of the building of the Temple of Solomon is different to the biblical story in that their version has the temple unfinished whereas in the Old Testament, the temple is completed although it was eventually destroyed. The Templars may well have incorporated the idea of an unfinished temple as a symbol of an order which was broken up and forced underground but which was and still is working towards a specific goal. There are several different versions of what that goal may be. Dan Brown and the authors of "Holy Blood, Holy Grail" would assert that the Templars and the shadowy masterminds pulling the strings behind the scenes were the guardians of the blood line of Christ. In this version the legendary Templar wealth was either a metaphor for the astounding and earth-shattering discovery that Christ had a wife and child, or it was a result of blackmailing the church with the threat of revealing this knowledge.

Most scholars acknowledge that the Templar wealth was accumulated in the rather more prosaic methods outlined earlier in this chapter. But it brings us to another interesting link between the Freemasons and the Templars, which is the antagonistic relationship they both have had with the Catholic Church.

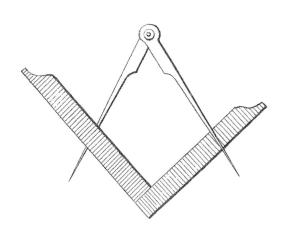

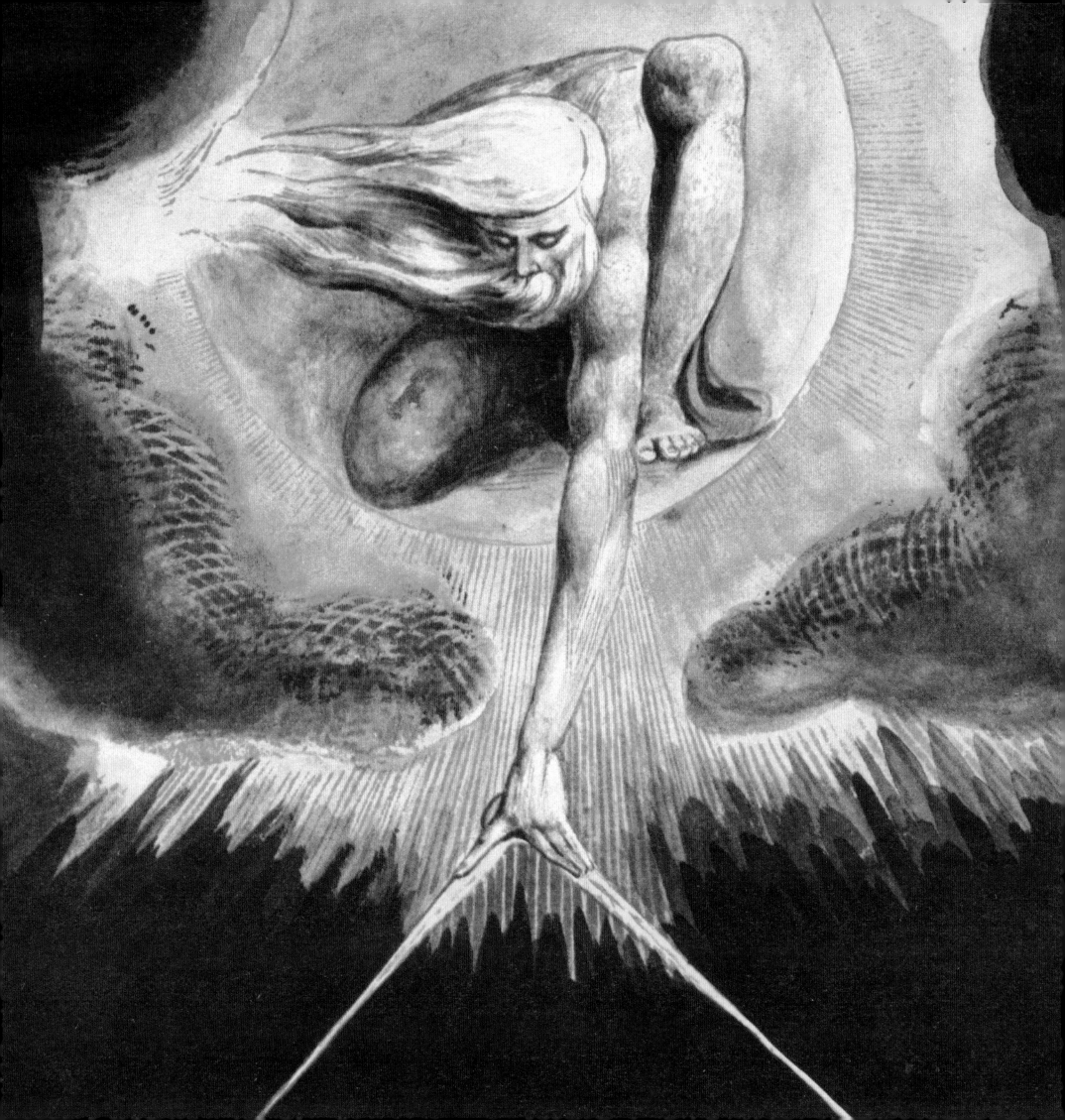

chapter 4

PERHAPS NOWHERE IS THE HOSTILITY OF THE CATHOLIC CHURCH TOWARDS FREEMASONRY BETTER ILLUSTRATED THAN IN HUMANUM GENUS, THE ENCYCLICAL OF POPE LEO XIII PROMULGATED IN 1884. IT IS A RATHER LENGTHY AND VERBOSE DOCUMENT BUT IT IS WORTH CITING HERE ALMOST IN ITS ENTIRETY TO REVEAL THE FERVOR AND RELIGIOUS ZEAL WITH WHICH THE POPE DENOUNCED THE MASONS AND ADMONISHED THE FAITHFUL TO DO THEIR UTMOST TO GUARD AGAINST THEIR SPREADING INFLUENCE.

William Blake's (1757-1827), image of the Creation. With the use of huge callipers he depicts God as the Creator set within the framework of the blazing sun.

THE MASONIC SECT

In our days however those who follow the evil one seem to conspire and strive all together under the guidance and with the help of that society which they call Free-Masons. Not dissimulating their intentions, they vie in attacking the power of God; they openly and ostensibly strive to damage the Church, with the purpose to deprive thoroughly if possible Christian people of the benefits brought by the Savior Jesus Christ...

The purpose and aim of the Masonic sect having been discovered from plain evidence, from the cognition of causes, its laws, rites and commentaries having

come to light and been made known by the additional depositions of the associated members, this Apostolic See denounced and openly declared that the sect of Masons is established against law and honesty, and is equally a danger to Christianity as well as to society; and threatening those heavy punishments which the Church uses against the guilty ones, she forbade the society, and ordered that none should give his name to it...

But the event justified the prudence of our predecessors, and this is the most important. Nay, their paternal care did not always and everywhere succeed, either because of the simulation and shrewdness of the Masons themselves, or through the inconsiderate levity of others whose duty

Pope Leo XIII

required of them strict attention. Hence in a century and a half the sect of Masons grew beyond expectation; and creeping audaciously and deceitfully among the various classes of the people, it grew to be so powerful that now it seems the only dominating power in the States...

For these reasons when we first succeeded in the government of the Church, we saw and felt very clearly the necessity of opposing so great and evil with the full weight of our authority.

Now after the example of our predecessors we intend to turn our attention to the Masonic society, to its whole doctrine, to its intentions, acts, and feelings, in order to illustrate more and more this wicked force and stop the spread of this contagious disease.

Enlightened thinkers were anathema to the Church.

Church

There are several sects of men, which though different in name, customs, forms and origins are identical in aim and sentiment with Masonry. It is the universal center from which they all spring, and to which they all return. Although in our days these seem to no longer care to hide in darkness, but hold their meetings in the full light and under the eyes of their fellow-men and publish their journals openly, yet they deliberate and preserve the habits and customs of secret societies. Nay, there are in them many secrets which are by law carefully concealed not only from the profane, but also from many associated, viz., the last and intimate intentions, the hidden

Early medieval illuminated manuscript

and unknown chiefs, the hidden and secret meetings, the resolutions and methods and means by which they will be carried into execution. Hence the difference of rights and of duties among the members; hence the distinction of orders and grades and the severe discipline by which they are ruled. The initiated must promise, nay take an oath that they will never at any way or at any time, disclose their fellow members and the emblems by which they are known, or expose their doctrines. So by false appearance but with the same kind of simulation the Masons chiefly strive as once did the Manicheans to hide and to admit no witnesses but their own. They seek skilfully hiding places, assuming the appearance of literary men or philosophers, associated for the purpose of erudition; they have always ready on their tongues the speech of cultivated urbanity, and proclaim their charity toward the poor; they look for improvement of the masses, to extend the benefits of social comfort to as many of mankind as possible. Those purposes though they may be true, yet are not the only ones. Besides those who are chosen to join the society must promise and swear to obey the leaders and teachers with great respect and trust; to be ready to do whatever is told them, and accept death and the most horrible punishment if they disobey. In fact some who have betrayed the secrets or disobeyed an order are punished with death so skilfully and so audaciously that the murder escaped the investigations of the police. Therefore reason and truth show that the society of which we speak is contrary to honest and natural justice.

There are other and clear arguments to show that this society is not in agreement with honesty. No matter how great the skill with which men conceal it, it is impossible that the cause should not appear in its effects. "A good tree cannot yield bad fruits nor a bad tree good ones." Masonry generates bad fruits mixed with great bitterness. From the evidence above mentioned we find its aim, which is the desire of overthrowing all the religious and social orders introduced by Christianity, and building a new one according to its taste, based on the foundation and laws of naturalism...

Now it is the principle of naturalists, as the name itself indicates, that human nature and human reason in everything must be our teacher and guide. Having once settled this, they are careless of their duties toward God, or they pervert them with false opinions and errors. They deny that anything has been revealed by God; they do not admit any religious dogma and truth but what human intelligence can comprehend; they do not allow any teacher to be believed on his official authority. Now it being the special duty of the Catholic Church and her duty only, to keep the doctrines received from God and the authority of teaching with all the heavenly means necessary to salvation and preserve them integrally incorrupt, hence the attacks and rage of the enemies are turned against her.

Now if one watches the proceedings of the Masons, in respect of religion especially, where they are more free to do what they like, it will appear that they carry faithfully into execution the tenets of the naturalists. They work, indeed, obstinately to the end that neither the

teaching nor the authority of the Church may have any influence; and therefore they preach and maintain the full separation of the Church from the State. So law and government are wrested from the wholesome and divine virtue of the Catholic Church, and they want, therefore, by all means to rule States independent of the institutions and doctrines of the Church.

To drive off the Church as a sure guide is not enough; they add persecutions and insults. Full licence is given to attack with impunity, both by words and print and teaching, the very foundations of the Catholic religion; the rights of the Church are violated; her divine privileges are not respected. Her action is restricted as much as possible; and that by virtue of laws apparently not too violent but made on purpose to check her freedom. Laws odiously partial against the clergy are passed so as to reduce its number and its means. The ecclesiastical revenue is in a thousand ways tied up and religious associations abolished and dispersed.

But the war wages more ardently against the Apostolic See and the Roman Pontiff. He was under a false pretext deprived of the temporal power, the stronghold of his rights and of his freedom; he was next reduced to an iniquitous condition, unbearable for its numberless burdens until it has come to this, that the Sectarians say openly what they had already in secret devised for a long time, viz., that the very spiritual power of the Pope ought to be taken away, and the divine institution of the Roman Pontificate ought to disappear from the world. If other arguments were needed for this, it would

be sufficiently demonstrated by the testimony of many who often in times bygone and even lately declared it to be the real supreme aim of the Freemasons to persecute with untamed hatred, Christianity, and that they will never rest until they see cast to the ground all religious institutions established by the Pope.

If the sect does not openly require its members to throw away of Catholic faith, this tolerance, far from injuring the Masonic schemes, is useful to them. Because this is, first, an easy way to deceive the simple and unwise ones and it is contributing to proselytize. By opening their gates to persons of every creed they promote, in fact, the great modern error of religious indifference and of the parity of all worships, the best way to annihilate every religion, especially the Catholic, which, being the only true one cannot be joined with others without enormous injustice...

It is true, Freemasons generally admit the existence of God; but they admit themselves that this persuasion for them is not firm, sure. They do not dissimulate that in the Masonic family the question of God is a principle of great discord; it is even known how they lately had on this point serious disputes. It is a fact that the sect leaves to the members full liberty of thinking about God whatever they like, affirming or denying His existence. Those who boldly deny His existence are admitted as well as those who like the Pantheists, admit God but ruin the idea of Him, retaining an absurd caricature of the divine nature, destroying its reality. Now as soon as this supreme

The risen Christ appears to Mary Magdalene.
The Gospel according to St. John.

Moses being presented with the Ten Commandments while the Israelites await his return from Mount Sinai. The tablets were housed in the innermost sanctum of King Solomon's Temple.

foundation is pulled down and upset, many natural truths must need go down too, as the free creations of this world, the universal government of providence, immortality of soul, fixture, and eternal life...

These principles once taken away by the Freemasons as by the naturalists, immediately natural ethics has no more where to build or to rest. The only morality which Freemasons admit, and by which they would like to bring up youth, is that which they call civil and independent, or the one which ignores every religious idea. But how poor, uncertain, and variable at every breath of passion is this morality, is demonstrated by the sorrowful fruits which partially already appear. Nay, where it has been freely dominating, having banished Christian education, probity and integrity of manners go down, horrible and monstrous opinions raise their head, and crimes grow with fearful audacity. This is deplored by everybody, and by those who are compelled by evidence and yet would not like to speak so...

What we have said may be confirmed by things of which it is not easy to think or speak. As these shrewd and malicious men do not find more servility and docility than in souls already broken and subdued by the tyranny of the passions, there have been in the Masonic sect some who openly said and proposed that the multitudes should be urged by all means and artifice into license, so that they should afterward become an easy instrument for the most daring enterprise.

For domestic society the doctrine of almost all naturalists is that marriage is only a civil contract, and may be lawfully broken by the will of the contracting parties; the State has power over the matrimonial bond. In the education of the children no religion must be applied, and when grown up every one will select that which he likes.

Now Freemasons accept these principles without restriction; and not only do they accept them, but they endeavor to act so as to bring them into moral and practical life...

The sect of the Masons aims unanimously and steadily at the possession of the education of children. They understand that a tender age is easily bent, and that there is no more useful way of preparing for the state such citizens as they wish. Hence, in the instruction and education of children, they do not leave to the ministers of the Church any part either in directing or watching them. In many places they have gone so far that children's education is all in the hands of laymen; and from moral teaching every idea is banished of those holy and great duties which bind together man and God.

The principles of social science follow. Here naturalists teach that men have all the same rights, and are perfectly equal in condition; that every man is naturally independent; that no one has a right to command others; that it is tyranny to keep men subject to any other authority than that which emanates from themselves. Hence the people are sovereign; those who rule have no authority but by the commission and concession of the people; so that they can be deposed, willing or unwilling, according to the wishes of the people. The origin of all rights and civil duties is in the people or in the state, which is ruled according to the new principles of liberty. The State must be godless; no reason why one religion ought to be preferred to another; all to be held in the same esteem.

Now it is well known that Freemasons approve these maxims, and that they wish to see governments shaped on this pattern and model needs no demonstration. It is a long time indeed that they have worked with all their strength and power openly for this, making thus an easy way for those, not a few, more audacious and bold in evil, who meditate the communion and equality of all goods after having swept away from the world every distinction of social goods and conditions.

From these few hints it is easy to understand what is the Masonic sect and what it wants. Its tenets contradict so evidently human reason that nothing can be more perverted. The desire of destroying the religion and church established by God, with the promise of immortal life, to try to revive, after eighteen centuries, the manners and institutions of paganism, is great foolishness and bold impiety. No less horrible or unbearable is it to repudiate the gifts granted through His adversaries.

In this foolish and ferocious attempt, one recognizes that untamed hatred and rage of revenge kindled against Jesus Christ in the heart of Satan.

The other attempt in which the Masons work so much, viz., to pull down the foundations of morality, and become co-operators of those who, like brutes, would see that become lawful which they like, is nothing but to urge mankind into the most abject and ignominious degradation...

That the State ought to profess religious indifference and neglect God in ruling society, as if God did not exist, is a foolishness unknown to the very heathen, who had so deeply rooted in their mind and in their heart, not only the idea of God, but the necessity also of public worship, that they supposed it to be easier to find a city without any foundation than without any God. And really human society, from which nature has made us, was instituted by God, the author of the same nature, and from Him emanates, as from its source and principle, all this everlasting abundance of numberless goods. As, then, the voice of nature tells us to worship God

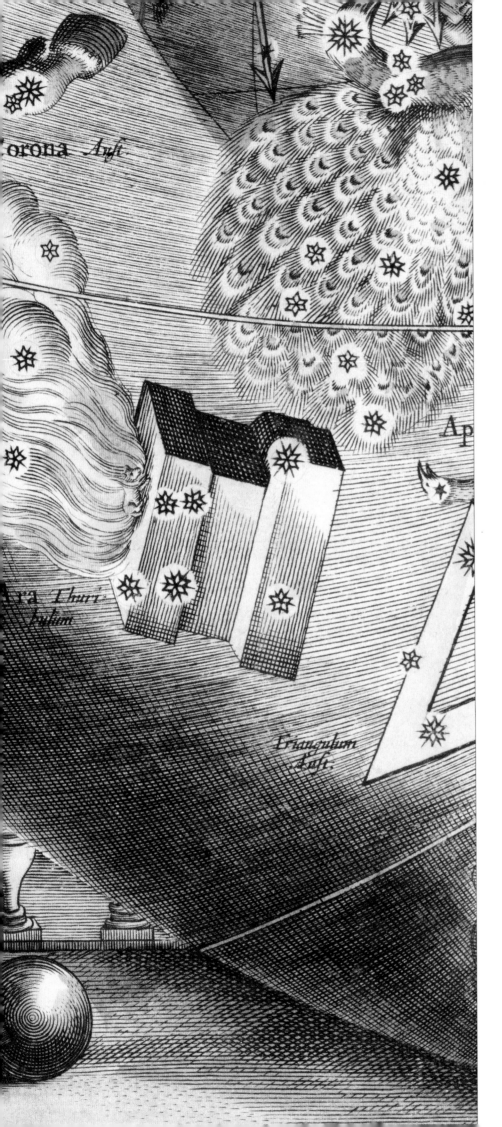

In the seventeenth century many of the
emerging generation of new scientists, such
as these astronomers, were Freemasons

with religious piety, because we have received from Him life and the goods which accompany life, so, for the same reasons, people and States must do the same. Therefore those who want to free society from any religious duty are not only unjust but unwise and absurd...

The turbulent errors which we have mentioned must inspire governments with fear; in fact suppose the fear of God in life and respect for divine laws to be despised, the authority of the rulers allowed and authorized would be destroyed, rebellion would be left free to popular passions, and universal revolution and subversion must necessarily come. This subversive revolution is the deliberate aim and open purpose of the numerous communistic and socialistic associations. The Masonic sect has no reason to call itself foreign to their purpose, because Masons promote their designs and have with them common capital principles. If the extreme consequences are not everywhere reached in fact, it is not the merit of the sect nor owing to the will of the members, but of that divine religion which cannot be extinguished and of the most select part of society, which, refusing to obey secret societies, resists strenuously their immoderate efforts...

Freemasons, insinuating themselves under pretence of friendship into the hearts of Princes, aim to have them powerful aids and accomplices to overcome Christianity, and in order to excite them more actively they calumniate the Church as the enemy of royal privileges and power. Having thus become confidant and sure, they get great influence in the government of States, resolve yet to shake the foundations of the thrones, and persecute, calumniate, or banish those sovereigns who refuse to rule as they desire.

By these arts flattering the people, they deceive them. Proclaiming all the time public prosperity and liberty; making multitudes believe that the Church is the cause of the iniquitous servitude and misery in which they are suffering, they deceive people and urge on the masses craving for new things against both powers. It is, however, true that the expectations of hoped-for advantages is greater than the reality; and poor people, more and more oppressed, see in their misery those comforts vanish which they might have easily and abundantly found in organized Christian society.

It would therefore be more according to civil wisdom and more necessary to universal welfare that Princes and Peoples, instead of joining with the Freemasons against the Church, should unite with the Church to resist the Freemasons' attacks.

At all events, the presence of such a great evil, already too much spread, it is our duty, venerable brethren, to find a remedy. And as we know that in the virtue of divine religion, the more hated by Masons as it is the more feared, chiefly consists the best and most solid of efficient remedy, we think that against the common enemy one must have recourse to this wholesome strength.

We, by our authority, ratify and condemn, confirm all things which the Roman Pontiffs, our predecessors

have ordered to check the purposes and stop the efforts of the Masonic sect, and all these which they establish to keep off or withdraw the faithful from such societies. And here, trusting greatly to the good will of the faithful, we pray and entreat each of them, as they love their own salvation, to make it a duty of conscience not to depart from what has been on this point prescribed by the Apostolic See.

We entreat and pray you, venerable brethren, who co-operate with us, to root out this poison, which spreads widely among the nations. It is your duty to defend the glory of God and the salvation of souls. Keeping before your eyes those two ends, you shall lack neither in courage nor in fortitude. To judge which may be the more efficacious means to overcome difficulties and obstacles belongs to your prudence. Yet as we find it agreeable to our ministry to point out some of the most useful means, the first thing to do is to strip from the Masonic sect its mask and show it as is, teaching orally and by pastoral letters the people about the frauds used by these societies to flatter and entice, the perversity of its doctrines, and the dishonesty of its works. As our predecessors have many times declared, those who love the Catholic faith and their own salvation must be sure that they cannot give their names for any reason to the Masonic sect without sin. Let no one believe a simulated honesty. It may seem to some that Masons never impose

Galileo Galilei was an Italian scientist who constructed a telescope with which he studied lunar craters, and discovered four moons revolving around Jupiter. His promotion of the Copernican theory led to his arrest.

anything openly contrary to faith or to morals, but as the scope and nature is essentially bad in these sects, it is not allowed to give one's name to them or to help them in any way...

In order more easily to reach the end, we recommend to your faith and watchfulness the youth, the hope of civil society. In the good education of the same place a great part of your care. Never believe you have watched or done enough in keeping youth from those masters from whom the contagious breath of the sect is to be feared. Insist that parents, and spiritual directors in teaching the catechism may never cease to admonish appropriately children and pupils of the wicked nature of these sects, that they may also learn in time the various fraudulent arts which their propagators use to entice. Those who prepare children for first communion will do well if they persuade them to promise not to give their names to any society without asking their parents' or their pastor's or their confessor's advice.

But we understand how our common labor would not be sufficient to outroot this dangerous seed from the field of the Lord, if the Heavenly Master of the vineyard is not to this effect granting to us His generous help. We must, then, implore His powerful aid with anxious fervor equal to the gravity of the danger and to the greatness of the need. Inebriated by its prosperous success, Masonry is insolent, and seems to have no more limits to its

pertinacity. Its sectaries bound by an iniquitous alliance and secret unity of purpose, they go hand in hand and encourage each other to dare more and more for evil. Such a strong assault requires a strong defence. We mean that all the good must unite in a great society of action and prayers...

Let us invoke for this purpose the meditation of Mary, the Virgin Mother of God, that against the impious sects in which one sees clearly revived the contumacious pride, the untamed perfidy, the simulating shrewdness of Satan, she may show her power, she who triumphed over him since conception...

Given at Rome, near Saint Peter, the 20th of April 1884, the seventh year of our pontificate.

The pope's emphatic use of language leaves no room for mistaking his dim view of Freemasonry. He uses words like "kingdom of Satan", "evils", "wicked force", "contagious disease", "horrible and monstrous opinions", "fearful audacity", "shrewd and malicious men."

Although it may be tempting to make the deduction that the ancient enmity between the Templars and the Catholic Church has resurfaced in Freemasonry after surviving underground for nearly five hundred years, such a theory can only ever rest on pure speculation. What can be asserted without doubt is that Freemasonry and the Catholic Church are and probably always will

NICOLAVS COPERNICVS
Mathematicus.

Quid tum? si mihi terra mouetur, Sol, qui escit,
Ac coelum: constat calculus inde meus.
M. D. XLI.

Copernicus was a Polish astronomer and mathematician who was a proponent of the view of an Earth in daily motion about its axis and in yearly motion around a stationary sun. This theory profoundly altered later workers' view of the universe, but was rejected by the Catholic Church.

be ideologically opposed because of the fundamental principles each of them holds.

Freemasonry insists that a potential candidate profess a belief in a deity but it leaves the nature of that deity up to the individual, hence putting the world's religions on an equal footing.

Pope Leo complains that "By opening their gates to persons of every creed they promote, in fact, the great modern error of religious indifference and of the parity of all worships, the best way to annihilate every religion, especially the Catholic, which, being the only true one cannot be joined with others without enormous injustice."

Because of Catholicism's insistence on being the one true faith, it cannot tolerate a society which says that all faiths are equally valid and each religion is only ever one aspect of the divine source from which the universe emanates.

Of course many of the pope's arguments seem hopelessly out of date to our modern minds. For example, we would not sympathize with his complaint that the Masons want to take the education of children out of the hands of the priesthood. Nor would we agree when he so strongly criticizes the prevailing current of intellectual thought deriving from the naturalists and the new social sciences. He complains that "naturalists teach that men have all the same rights, and are perfectly equal in condition; that every man is naturally independent; that no one has a right to command others; that it is a tyranny to keep men subject to any other authority than that which emanates from themselves. Hence the people are sovereign; those who rule have no authority but by the commission and concession of the people; so that they can be deposed, willing or unwilling, according to the wishes of the people."

His anger here is directed not at Freemasonry itself but at the emergence of democracy and the subsequent waning of the autocratic powers of the Church for which he blames the Masons. But really he is trying to hold back the tide of history and the increasing demands of a global population for the same rights that were won by the Americans in the War of Revolution a century earlier.

It must be borne in mind that because Pope Leo XIII had recently lost the Papal States to the new kingdom of Italy, he was the first pontiff for centuries without the title and powers of a king. The world was changing and the powers of the church, once so far-reaching were in serious decline. It seems as though the Masons offer a convenient peg on which to hang all the causes for the "evils" of the world, like democracy and the separation of Church and State.

But there may be other reasons for the mutual antipathy and distrust between the Masons and the Catholic Church, which goes back to the days of secret Masonry before the society declared itself in 1717.

To understand this the great importance that Freemasonry places on the science of Geometry must

George Washington, an active Mason for most of his life, commissioned Pierre Charles L'Enfant to draw up the original plan for Washington D.C.

be borne in mind. Such is the reverence for this pursuit that the letter G plays a crucial role in the symbolism of allegorical Masonry, for it is with the laws of Geometry that man is able to appreciate the laws of the universe and comprehend his place within it.

Now it just so happens that with this very science Galileo Galiei had come to a conclusion that directly contradicted the teachings of the Church, namely that Copernicus was right in asserting that the sun revolves around the earth. This challenge to the spiritual and temporal authority of the Church could not be tolerated and in an era when the Church had the power to punish such heresies, Galileo had to recant his views and live out his days under house arrest. Unfortunately for the Church the interest in celestial geometry or astronomy as we know it today could not be suppressed despite the appearance of it having disappeared.

It is now widely acknowledged that those with an interest in the new sciences went underground and met in secret in an "invisible college" which as time went by became confident enough to ask for a Royal Charter and was known ever after as the Royal Society.

Fifty-five years later, when Freemasonry no longer felt the need for secrecy, it became apparent that nearly every member and founding member of the Royal Society was a Freemason. Hence we can appreciate that an atmosphere of mutual mistrust and suspicion had existed between the Catholic Church and Freemasonry ever since its declaration in 1717 and probably well before.

But it was in America that the biggest wedge was driven between the Church and State and the influence of the Masons there cannot be underestimated. The most influential names in the American Revolution is a roll call of the most prominent Freemasons: George Washington, Benjamin Franklin, James Monroe, Alexander Hamilton, Paul Revere, John Paul Jones and Benedict Arnold. And many of the subsequent presidents were Freemasons: Andrew Jackson, James K. Polk, James Buchanan, Andrew Johnson, James A. Garfield, Theodore Roosevelt, William Howard Taft, Warren G. Harding, Franklin D. Roosevelt, Harry S. Truman, Lyndon Johnson, Gerald Ford and honorary brother Ronald Reagan.

The first amendment guaranteeing that the "Congress shall make no law respecting an establishment of religion, or prohibiting the free exercise thereof" reflects the tolerance of the Masonic view towards matters of faith. It is unlikely to be coincidence that the Freemasons were also rumored to have masterminded the French Revolution and France is notable for the absence of religious instruction in state schools.

With such an influence, whether real or imagined, it is scarcely surprising that the Catholic Church was so scathing in its attack on Freemasonry.

An early design of the Pyramid and the Eye
which features on the American dollar bill

chapter 5

PERHAPS THE WORST MOMENT IN THE HISTORY OF FREEMASONRY CAME IN 1981 WHEN ITS NAME WAS LINKED TO ONE OF THE BIGGEST CORRUPTION SCANDALS TO HIT ITALY. SO FAR-REACHING WERE ITS IMPLICATIONS THAT IT BROUGHT DOWN THE COALITION GOVERNMENT UNDER ARNALDO FORLANI AND WAS EVEN HELD TO BE LINKED TO THE DEATH OF POPE JOHN PAUL I.

The 'Eye of God' watches over humanity

The double helix staircase in the Vatican, designed in 1932 by Giuseppe Momo

Bad

The controversy centers on an Italian lodge of Freemasons known as P2, which is the abbreviation of Propaganda Due. It took its name from a lodge that had been formed by the Grand Orient of Italy in Turin over a century earlier, which rapidly established itself as pre-eminent in the country, including many nobles and even royalty among its brethren.

The modern P2 was formed by Giordano Gamberini in 1966 with the stated aim of establishing a nexus of powerful men who could further the cause of Freemasonry. A Master Mason from the town of Arezzo in Tuscany was chosen to head up the lodge and before long the Italian Grand Orient was so concerned at the directions his activities were taking the lodge that he officially severed all ties and publicly disowned them. The man who had caused such consternation was Licio Gelli, a prominent businessman and manufacturer who had a somewhat chequered past, to say the least.

He had cut his teeth fighting alongside the fascists in the Spanish Civil War in the Italian Blackshirt Division and during World War II he was a liaison officer with the Nazis rising to the rank of Oberleutnant in the S.S. After the war he faced a war crimes trial accused of murdering and torturing patriots, but he had worked for both sides, and Communist allies made sure that the case against him collapsed.

For a while he was involved with

Pope Paul VI

arranging "ratlines" to help Nazis fleeing justice escape to South America. When this was no longer lucrative he went to Argentina and aligned himself first with General Peron and then with the right-wing junta that ousted him. When General Peron later returned to exile from power, several witnesses confirmed that he kneeled in gratitude before Gelli.

Arezzo's Piazza Grande, Tuscany, Italy

and influence, joined a lodge in 1963. Rising to the rank of Master Mason and hence becoming eligible to lead a lodge himself he leapt at the chance given him by Gamberini.

It quickly became apparent however that he had absolutely no interest in the moral self-improvement central to Masonic ritual but wanted to use the ties of allegiance to consolidate his own Italian power base.

As the head of Raggruppamento Gelli–P2, he targeted retired senior members of the Armed Forces and through them he gained introductions to active service heads of staff. He was by now a master in the art of corruption and he knew that the way to power lay through knowledge.

Publicity

This was a man who as the Argentinian economic adviser to Italy purchased Exocet missiles for Argentina while simultaneously working for S.I.D, the Italian Army Intelligence and selling information to both the C.I.A and the Soviet Union.

The Freemasons had been proscribed under Mussolini but they were rehabilitated under the post-war Democratic government and Licio Gelli, never one to pass up an opportunity to exploit a new source of power

Whenever a new member joined P2, he was obliged to show his loyalty by bringing with him information that would compromise not only himself but others in his professional or political sphere. Gelli now had a hold on the new member and when he threatened the contacts with blackmail he invariably gained yet more initiates and more contacts and so the web was spun ever wider.

Statues of Popes and Saints line the ornate facade of the Vatican

Another cunning ruse was to find out the short-lists of candidates for promotion to the very top positions in industry and finance, call each one and tell him that he intended to use his influence to secure the job for him and then all he had to do was sit back and wait for the successful candidate to join his lodge in gratitude.

As the Venerable Master of the Lodge, Gelli was the only one who knew the full extent of the circle of influence he had consolidated. P2 was divided into seventeen cells, each with its own group leader and these group leaders only knew the membership of their own cell.

By the 1970s his infiltration of Italian aristocratic, administrative, executive, judicial, financial and military establishments was complete and Italy was well and truly rotten to the core.

Among the men who had sworn an oath of allegiance to him were: the Commander of the Armed Forces Giovani Torrisi, and seven other admirals, thirty generals and three heads of the secret service (the Defence Chief of Staff, the Chief of Military Counter-Espionage and the Chief of National Security), nineteen judges, the Head of Italy's Financial Police Orazio Giannini, the editor of Il Corriere della Sera, the leading newspaper, top industrialists and bankers, cabinet ministers and politicians from every party except the Communist Party.

It has since become apparent that the stated aim of P2 was a secret right wing power base which would control the country from behind the scenes unless the Communists came to power in which case they would use the army to arrange a coup d'etat.

Despite being exposed to the glare of public scrutiny after the scandal which rocked the nation in 1981, there exist to this day chapters of P2 that maintain links with military regimes and neo-fascist organizations around the world and they have been very active in Latin America, especially in Bolivia where they liased with the private army known as the "Fiances of Death" established by Klaus Barbie. In Argentina the creator of the infamous "Triple A Death Squads", Jose Lopez Rega, was a member of P2.

It is not clear who was Gelli's main point of entry into the otherwise almost hermetically sealed world of the Vatican. Despite the papal pronouncement that membership of Freemasonry was not only incompatible with the Catholic faith it would actually result in excommunication, there were several prominent officials within the Vatican who were members of P2.

Gelli probably infiltrated the Vatican through one of his most useful P2 brethren, Umberto Ortolani, who was known as "the Puppet Master." A successful businessman and lawyer, he had links with the Vatican that went back as early as the 1950s. He was so close to Cardinal Lercaro that people thought, and Ortolani did not correct them, that they were cousins.

During the run-up to the election of Pope Paul VI, Ortolani offered his villa as a venue for a meeting attended by a faction who wanted to ensure the election of their candidate and when they were successful, Ortolani was granted the Vatican award of "Gentleman of his Holiness" in gratitude. He was subsequently able

Evita and General Juan Perón
of Argentina

to get Gelli affiliated to the Knights of Malta and the Holy Sepulcher, the order descended from the Knights Hospitallers, which is recognized as a sovereign state by the Vatican. This was all the more remarkable because Gelli was not a practicing Catholic.

Some prominent officials may have believed that the Vatican and P2 had a common cause in their fear and loathing of Communism. Gelli's favorite phrase was a quote by cardinal Hinsley of Westminster who said in 1935: "If Fascism goes under, God's cause goes under with it."

But they would have been shocked at the methods P2 used to achieve their goal of preventing Italy falling into Communist hands. Throughout the sixties and seventies there was a widespread bombing campaign that was almost certainly orchestrated by P2, hoping to blame the outrages on the Communists and thus turn public opinion against them.

This was not however the only way that violence was used to further their cause. In July 1976 a magistrate was gunned down in the street to stop the investigation which he was conducting into the link between a neo-Fascist group called National Vanguard and P2.

In the late 1960s Michele Sindona joined P2. He was known as the "Shark" by his friends in recognition of his shrewd financial wheeling and dealing, so what his enemies called him is anybody's guess! He had close links with both the Sicilian Mafia and

the five New York Cosa Nostra families Colombo, Bonanno, Lucchese, Genovese and in particular the Gambinos. He used his financial acumen to launder Mafia money earned dealing in drugs, prostitution, gambling, protection and racketeering.

Born in Sicily he earned his stripes on the Black Market during World War II. Accounting and tax law soon became his speciality, skills which were indispensable to the cash-rich Mafia and he was able to invest their money and move it in and out of Italy without accruing any tax burdens.

With Mafia money he began to buy banks and set up holding companies as the best way to illegally transfer funds out of the country. Realizing the potential goldmine that the Vatican represented, he curried favor with the Archbishop of Milan by putting up over two million dollars (of Mafia money!) for an old people's home and soon the diocese was relying almost exclusively upon him for financial advice.

Soon enough, he had cultivated the friendships of the Administrative Secretary of the Vatican Bank and Monsignor Sergio Guerri the man in charge of the Special Administration, which looked after the Vatican investments around the world.

A former employee of Sindona's who turned State evidence against his boss described a brokerage company he helped set up for Sindona thus:

"These foreign currency black

General Francisco Franco
of Spain

The Sistine Chapel, painted by Michelangelo between 1536
and 1541, is centered on the dominant picture of Christ, captured in
the moment before the verdict of the Last Judgement is uttered.

operations, a vast illegal export of capital, took place daily and large figures were involved. The technique was really the most coarse and criminal which can be imagined."

Money was stolen from the accounts of depositors, moved to an account held by the Vatican bank and then moved again to another account in the Banque de Financement (Finabank) owned by Sindona in Switzerland, minus a 15% commission of course.

Here the money was used to speculate on the financial markets and the losses (which by the time the Swiss bank inspectors put a stop to it amounted to over $30 million) were financed by a shell company called Liberfinco (Liberian Financial Company.)

The modern source of the Vatican wealth goes back to a payment made by Mussolini to the Vatican under the terms of the Lateran agreement. In exchange for Vatican support, Mussolini agreed to guarantee religious teaching in schools and not to pass laws, which would contravene the tenets of the Catholic faith. In addition he recognized the Vatican as a sovereign state and undertook to pay "the sum of 750 million lire and to hand over at the same time Consolidated 5 per cent State Bonds to the bearer for the nominal value of one billion lire."

The Special Administration was created to invest the money.

The Administration of Religious Works had been created in 1887 by Pope Pius XII to administer money for charitable causes. In 1942 its name was changed to the Institute for Religious Works (I.O.R.) and it was soon known unofficially as the Vatican Bank. Its charitable purpose became rather muddied however when Bishop Paul Marcinkus took the helm. Known as the "Gorilla" for his 6 ft 3 in., sixteen stone frame, he came to the pope's attention when he saved him from being crushed by a crowd that surged forward to greet him.

The Vatican had decided to sell its huge share portfolio, which had become an embarrassment and the source of much investigative journalism, which had unearthed investments in pharmaceutical companies that made the contraceptive pill, and arms manufacturers. There were growing calls for the church to return to the simplicity and material poverty that was so central to the teachings of Christ.

Articles condemning the materialism of the Vatican started to appear such as this one in Il Mondo:

"Is it right for the Vatican to operate in markets like a speculator? Is it right for the Vatican to have a bank whose operations help the illegal transfer of capital from Italy to other countries? Is it right for that bank to assist Italians in evading tax?

The Church preaches equality but it does not seem to us that the best way to ensure equality is by evading taxes, which constitute the means by which the Lay State tries to promote the same equality."

The plan was for the Vatican to transfer their investments in the Italian financial markets to foreign markets, in particular the U.S.A and begin to invest in Eurodollar blue-chips and off-shore profits.

Sindona offered to take a large part of their portfolio including the shares in Societa Gerneral Immobiliare

Commander Giovani Torrisi

which had assets worth over half a billion dollars. The shares were paid for with money illegally converted from deposits at a bank he had acquired called Banca Privata Finanziaria and the deal was arranged by Umberto Ortolani, Licio Gelli's right hand man.

By now, Sindona had begun to manipulate the Milan Stock market with an associate called Roberto Calvi and such was their effect that the economy suffered and unemployment rose.

One single illegal kick-back given by Sindona to Calvi for buying shares that had been artificially elevated was said to have been as much $6.5 million at 1972 levels of inflation.

The link between P2, the Mafia and the Vatican was by now so inextricable that money was being cleaned on its way into Italy via the Vatican Bank.

Meanwhile Sindona turned his attention to America and after purchasing the Franklin National Bank of New York, which was the twentieth largest bank in America he tried to gain a foothold in the corridors of power of the world's largest economy by offering Richard Nixon's Presidential Campaign Chief Fund Raiser a suitcase containing a million dollars cash, "to show his faith in America."

Before long however the chickens were coming home to roost for the man that the Italian Prime Minister had once described as "The savior of the Lira". At the beginning of 1974 the Stock market went into decline and Il Crack Sindona as the Italian newspapers dubbed it began to appear. He had been using his banks to siphon off money for so long that a huge hole began to appear which he could no longer cover up. The U.S. Government was so alarmed at the prospect of the collapse of the Franklin Bank that they gave it unlimited access to the Federal Reserve. In Italy his Banca Privata was propped up with $128 million dollars but to no avail. In October of the same year both the Franklin and the Privata banks collapsed, costing the Federal Reserve Insurance Corporation over $2 billion, the worst disaster in American banking history.

It was now that Sindona's Masonic connections paid off for corrupt sources in the judiciary and the police force tipped off Gelli that Sindona was about to be arrested and he was able to flee the country. While Sindona was fighting extradition in America, another P2 member Roberto Calvi took over the business of speculating on behalf of Vatican Incorporated.

He had begun his financial career working for the

St. Peter's Square, Rome

Banco Ambrosiano in Milan, known as the Priest's Bank because a written deposition guaranteeing one's faith was required before one could use its services. Cardinal Archbishop of Milan banked there and board meetings were begun with prayers.

Calvi was another P2 member, variously known as the "Knight" and the "Paymaster" in recognition of his huge financial clout. He was also absolutely corrupt in his banking practice and soon enough the Banco Ambrosiano was involved in another scandal which rocked the foundations of the Vatican.

In 1963 he had formed a shell company known as Banco Ambrosiano

Holdings, which began borrowing money from banks around the world which it never had any intention of repaying. The Vatican Bank was by now inextricably linked with Calvi and indeed he would not have been able to get away with his crimes if it wasn't for the association with their prestigious name.

After Il Crack Sindona money became more difficult to borrow and his share price fell so he began to purchase his own shares at massively inflated prices thus illegally propping up the market value.

He covered this up by investing in shell companies in Latin America, Nicaragua, Peru and Panama, which were beyond the jurisdiction of the Bank of Italy. Eventually there were 17 of them in total, all owned by a Luxembourg Company, which was in turn owned by the Vatican Bank.

Greatly overvalued shares were offered as security for huge loans, some of which were diverted to Gelli, who purchased arms for the Argentinian Government in its war with Great Britain over the Falkland Islands.

In September 1978, Pope John Paul I had received a list of P2 members from a news agency calling itself L'Osservatore Politico (O.P), run by a journalist called Mino Pecorelli, a former member of P2 who had fallen out with Gelli. The list contained many senior figures in the Vatican, including the pope's own secretary. News of his resolve to replace the Freemasons with non-masons leaked out to Gelli and Calvi and would have been serious cause for concern. If Marckinkus were to be replaced with an honest man with no alliance to P2, the lid would be lifted on the scam that had been running so profitably for everyone involved.

The morning after the Pope had drawn up his list of proposed changes to the Vatican infrastructure which involved sweeping the household clean of P2 members, he was found dead in his bed.

Inside the Vatican corridors of power

The cause of death has never been established to anyone's satisfaction because no doctor would give his name to the certificate of death. Vatican officials gave the cause as heart attack due to myocardial infarction, despite the fact that this is impossible to diagnose without an autopsy and the pope was considered to be in good health. There were growing calls from the public for an autopsy, which the Vatican refused, claiming that a pope cannot be examined in this way although records show that in 1830 an autopsy was performed on a deceased pope.

One doctor interviewed at the time said that given the circumstances he would not have given his consent for the body to be buried. It was remembered that the Russian Orthodox Archbishop of Leningrad had been received by the pope only days before and had suddenly slumped forward in his chair and died. Rumors circulated that he had drunk a cup of coffee intended for Pope John Paul I. Within fourteen hours of the time of death the body had been embalmed thus rendering impossible any investigation into the use of poison.

The nun who was accustomed to take in a cup of coffee to the pope at 4:45 am, and who had discovered the body, asserted that he had a file of papers in his hands when she found him, despite the official version that he was reading the fifteenth century tract "The Imitation of Christ" by Thomas a Kempis. The papers, which many argue were the list of proposed changes within the Vatican were never seen again and the nun was packed off to a remote village in the north of Italy, far away from the media spotlight.

There were still more deaths to come however, with Pecorelli, the former and disgruntled member of P2, the next to die. Having attempted to blackmail Gelli about his involvement with the Communists, he received two bullets to the head, fired from within his mouth to indicate it was a punishment by the Sicilian Mafia for having a big mouth.

The influence of P2 was such that in an extraordinary example of corruption, the Head of Vigilance of the Bank of Italy, Mario Sarcinelli, and his Governor, Paolo Baffi, who were investigating Calvi, were actually arrested and thrown in jail. It was not until January 1980 that the charges were dropped and proved false and in the meantime they were not allowed to continue their investigation. The liquidator of Sindona's bank, Giorgio Ambrosoli was also gunned down in the street.

But then in 1981, Gelli's villa in Arezzo was raided by the Italian police and a list of 962 members of P2 was discovered. Suddenly this once shadowy and powerful elite was exposed to the unwelcome glare of publicity and the resultant furore brought down the Italian Government.

The investigation into the Calvi-Marckincus-Sindona triangle of fraud was intensified and Calvi was sentenced to four years' imprisonment. If anyone doubted that P2 still had influence despite the exposure, they were silenced when Calvi lodged an appeal against his sentence,

Michele Sindona

was freed on bail and then reinstated as the chairman of Banco Ambrosiano.

But time was running out for him. He was guilty of such serious financial fraud that in the end he was stealing even from himself. He must have known there was no way out for him when he left Italy with a forged passport and ended up in London. On the morning of June 17 1982, he was found hanging from scaffolding underneath Blackfriar's bridge with chunks of masonry in his pockets. There has been much controversy surrounding his death. Many people are convinced that he was murdered in accordance with Masonic ritual with a "cable-tow" around his neck "where the tide ebbs and flows twice in twenty-four hours."

Whatever happened to him, one should not underestimate a secret society that included amongst its number, three members of Cabinet, of which one was the Justice Minister, several former Prime Ministers and forty-three members of Parliament. Although largely broken up, the chairman of the commission appointed to investigate, said,

"P2 is by no means dead. It still has power. It is working in the institutions. It is moving in society. It has money, means and instruments still at its disposal. It still has fully operative power centers in South America. It is also still able to condition, at least in part, Italian political life."

  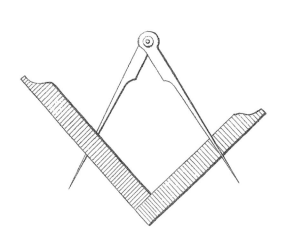

chapter 6

IN THE EARLY HOURS OF AUGUST 31 1888 AN UNIDENTIFIED HOMICIDAL MANIAC MURDERED AND MUTILATED A PROSTITUTE CALLED POLLY NICHOLLS AND BURST INTO THE COLLECTIVE CONSCIOUSNESS OF THE WORLD. HIS REIGN OF TERROR WOULD LAST FOR TEN WEEKS AND TO THIS DAY, DESPITE THE BEST EFFORTS OF THE METROPOLITAN AND CITY POLICE, HIS CRIMES REMAIN UNSOLVED.

THE FACT THAT HE WAS TO EVADE ARREST AND PROSECUTION HAS ALLOWED A VERITABLE INDUSTRY OF CONSPIRACY THEORIES TO GROW UP AROUND THE MYTH OF THE MAN KNOWN ONLY AS JACK THE RIPPER. ONE OF THESE THEORIES WAS TO BLACKEN THE NAME OF THE FREEMASONS BY ASSOCIATION AND PROVED TO BE AMONG THE WORST OF THE ACCUSATIONS LEVELLED AT THE BROTHERHOOD.

Was Jack the Ripper

This first crime, ghastly as it was only rated a mention on page three of the Daily Star but when he struck again a week later, he would make the front pages of every newspaper in the country. The second victim, Annie Chapman was a terminally ill woman, whose drinking and squalid life left her looking far older than her 47 years. Forced to make a living as a prostitute on the dark and dangerous streets of Whitechapel, she was a familiar face on the street corners and in the pubs. On the night of September 8th she was trying to make the four pence she needed for a bed in a cheap doss house, when she ran into the arms of Jack the Ripper. A porter on his way to work in Spitalfields Market found her in the back yard of a tenement block on Hanbury Street. Her throat had been slashed right back to the vertebrae

and she had been disembowelled. Her intestines were laid over her right shoulder.

The citizens of London were feverish with fear and panic. An unknown assailant was living among them, a fiend capable of the most monstrous desecration of the human body.

The Star proclaimed "London lies today under the spell of a great terror. A nameless reprobate (half beast, half man) is at large. The ghoul-like creature who stalks through the streets of London, stalking down his victim like a Pawnee Indian, is simply drunk with blood, and would have much more."

For three weeks, London held its breath. Melville MacNaughton, head of CID, wrote in his memoirs

"No one who was living in London that autumn will forget the terror created by these murders... Even now I can recall the foggy evenings and hear again the raucous cries of the newspaper boys: "Another horrible murder, murder, mutilation in Whitechapel..." Such was the burden of their ghastly song and when the double murder of 30 September took place, no servant-maid deemed her life safe if she ventured out to post a letter after ten o'clock at night..."

The double murder of 30 September was especially significant because the Central News Agency had received a letter three days earlier from someone who signed himself Jack the Ripper, the first use of the now infamous moniker.

Letter with Jack the Ripper's signature, sent to Press Association, 28th September 1889

a ginger-bottle to write with but it went thick like glue and I can't use it. Red ink is fit enough I hope. The next job I do I shall clip the lady's ears off just for jolly wouldn't you? My knife's so nice and sharp I want to get to work straight away if I get a chance. Good Luck..."

Much has been made of the fact that in the three weeks since the last murder, interest in the case was flagging and this letter may have been an attempt by a journalist acting either alone or under the direction of an editor to revive public attention. The murders had been great business for the newspapers, and much of the reporting was tabloid journalism of the most lurid kind, which would make our modern gutter press look tame by comparison.

a Freemason?

"Dear Boss" it went. "I keep hearing the police have caught me, but they won't fix me just yet... I am down on whores and I shan't quit ripping them 'til I do get buckled. Grand work the last job was. I gave the lady no time to squeal. How can they catch me now? I love my work and want to start again. You will soon hear of me with my funny little games. I saved some of the proper red stuff in

Another letter received only a matter of hours after the murders may well be authentic as it taunts "Double event this time" and thus drastically reduces the number of people privy to this information.

Elizabeth Stride and Catherine Eddowes were the poor women brutally murdered that night. Elizabeth Stride or "Long Liz" as she was known to her friends was discovered with her

Annie and John Chapman, 1869. This is believed to be the only known photograph of any Whitechapel murder victims prior to death.

Catherine Eddowes

throat cut but no mutilations and it is possible that the killer was disturbed by a coachman returning from Westow Hill market where he had gone to sell jewellery. Forty-five minutes later the body of Catherine Eddowes was discovered, terribly mutilated in Mitre Square, just within the bounds of the City of London's Square Mile.

Strangely enough, Catherine Eddowes had only just been released from jail about an hour before she was murdered. She had been arrested for being drunk and disorderly on Aldgate High Street and was confined in a cell until she had slept it off. When she started singing, the sergeant on duty let her out so he could get some peace and quiet. She had identified herself as Mary Kelly to the arresting officer and this was to assume great significance for conspiracy theorists at a later date. But perhaps the most intriguing and potentially explosive twist to this otherwise sordid tale, was something that happened in the immediate aftermath of the double murder.

At five minutes to three that morning PC Alfred Long found in Goulston Street a torn piece of Catherine Eddowes' apron, which had apparently been used to clean the killer's blood-stained knife. Written in chalk, in a "good schoolboy's hand" on the wall just next to the spot, were the mysterious words "The Juwes are the men that will not be blamed for nothing."

Although the last murder was committed within the jurisdiction of the City Police, Goulston Street was within the bounds of the Metropolitan Police Force.

When the Chief Commissioner Sir Charles Warren arrived on the scene he immediately ordered the writing removed, citing his fears of an anti-Semitic riot. Suspicion had already fallen on the Jewish immigrant population that had recently come to the East End fleeing persecution in the Russian pogroms. Sir Charles' precaution may well have been justified, however he refused the City Police (who unlike the Metropolitan Police, owned a camera) permission to photograph the writing. Likewise he would not listen to the earnest entreaties of the detectives on the scene to simply cover up the message or remove only the offending word "Juwes".

This action has been deemed at best grossly incompetent and at worst highly suspicious. Having access to the handwriting would have proved of enormous value in authenticating the thousands upon thousands of letters that were pouring into the police and newspapers, purporting to come from the pen of the Ripper. It might also have led to a successful conviction if a suspect was ever detained. When Sir Charles rubbed off the message dawn was still a couple of hours away. Besides, the area could very easily have been cordoned off.

Questions were soon being asked as to the motive Sir Charles might have had in wanting to remove the seemingly innocuous words. Did he read something between the lines, which he did not want others to see, people who might also be able to decode the hidden message?

And it was not long before a motive was supplied.

Durward Street, London, c 1872

Grave of Mary Ann Nichols in Ilford Cemetery, London

Sir Charles was himself a leading Mason. As such he could not have failed to notice the deliberate misspelling of the word "Juwes". He would have recognized the veiled reference to Jubelo, Jubela and Jubelum known collectively as the "Juwes", who feature so heavily in the creation myths and rituals of the Freemasons.

"Oh that my throat had been cut across, my tongue torn out, and my body buried in the rough sands of the sea, at low water mark, where the tide ebbs and flows twice in twenty-four hours" cried Jubela when taken for the murder of Hiram Abiff, the architect of the temple.

"Oh that my left breast had been torn open and my heart and vitals taken from thence and thrown over my left shoulder" were the despairing words of Jubelo.

Jubelum: "O that my body had been severed in twain in the midst, and divided to the north and south, my bowels burnt to ashes in the center and the ashes scattered by the four winds of heaven."

Much has been made of the similarity of the Ripper mutilations to the oaths of initiation taken by Masons as they progress through the varying degrees of Craft Masonry. After all, the victims all had their throats cut across and were disembowelled, with their "vitals" thrown over by their shoulder.

And at first sight the murders do seem to have a ritualistic element to them. However on closer inspection, discrepancies begin to emerge, such as the fact that in the two instances where the bowels were placed by the head, they were placed by the right and not the left shoulder. This leads to the possible conclusion that the murderer was someone familiar with the rituals of Freemasonry, but not a Mason himself, for the varying procedures of the initiation ceremonies are nothing if not exact and any Mason worth his salt would have known them inside out.

There arose the theory that the murders may have been a deranged attempt to discredit the Freemasons. However this does not stand up to scrutiny because the connection between the Ripper murders and the Freemasons was not made until 1976 when Stephen Knight wrote "Jack the Ripper: The Final Solution"

Thus the throats may well have been cut because this was the most immediately effective way of silencing the victims, and the bowels may have been placed over the shoulders because they had to go somewhere while the murderer was going about his gruesome task.

Great Synagogue, Brick Lane, East London, c 1953

The story as presented in Stephen Knight's book is very compelling and contains all the elements of the most exciting fiction, both contemporary detective and Victorian melodrama. In fact it has become an inextricable part of the archetypal make-up of this otherwise rather sordid tale of homicidal mania. So pervasive is the influence that when Hollywood decided to revisit the story in 2002, a graphic novel by Alan Moore detailing exactly the same kind of conspiracy provided the source material.

Discovery of Alice Mckenzie's body from The Penny Illustrated Paper, July 1889

The basic premise is as follows:

In the early seventies a man named Joseph Sickert had made a series of startling allegations in a BBC series entitled "Jack the Ripper". He claimed to be the son of Walter Sickert the artist and a woman called Alice Margaret Crook. As a little boy his mother had told him to be very wary never to do anything to bring himself to the attention of the authorities, for his grandmother had suffered terribly at their hands and one of the family's servants had died a most horrific death. When he asked his father to elaborate he told him a thinly disguised fairy tale about a prince and a poor shop girl who had fallen in love and had a child together. They married in secret and were happy together for a while even though the prince was forced to live a double life. At some point the prince's family found out and forced them apart. The girl was confined in an asylum for the insane but a servant escaped with the child and disappeared.

When Joseph Sickert was older, his father told him the facts behind the story. As a painter of great renown he was asked by the Duke of Clarence's mother, Princess Alexandra, to introduce her son to the world of art and artistic circles. Prince Albert Victor, as he was also known, soon became good friends with Sickert and would often accompany him to his studio in Cleveland Street where he was introduced as Sickert's brother. Here he met one of Sickert's models, a young Catholic woman named Ann Elizabeth Crook, who worked in a shop opposite his studio on Cleveland Street in the West End of London.

She was very beautiful and they were soon in love. At a private ceremony in Saint Saviour's Chapel, witnessed only by very close friends, they married and soon a child was born.

When it was discovered that the heir to the throne had a legitimate daughter who was born of a Catholic mother, it was decided that the matter had to be hushed up. This was a time when the threat of revolution was in the air. The disaffected under-classes were being stirred into political ferment by socialist agitators and Ireland was pressing for home rule. London was rocked by a series of terrorist attacks perpetrated by the Fenian brotherhood of American Irish emigres, the most notable of which were the attempts to blow up the Houses of Parliament and the Tower of London.

Accordingly, Ann was taken away to Guy's Hospital where she was declared insane and her ravings that she was the wife of the Prince could be ascribed to the ravings of a poor deluded woman. Later she was taken to a hospital in Fulham Road where she was confined until her death in 1920.

With that part of the problem dealt with however, attention turned to what to do with those who had witnessed the marriage and now had to be silenced. Foremost amongst them was a friend called Mary Jane Kelly, who in some versions of the story took the girl away with her and

Mary Kelly at Miller's Court

Sir Melville MacNaughton

her and in other versions simply disappeared when the couple were separated.

In Knight's book, Mary Kelly tells four other women of this potentially explosive secret and they try to blackmail the Royal family in return for their silence. Whether she was unable to keep the secret, or whether the other women were killed to throw the investigators off the scent is pure conjecture, as indeed is the whole story, based as it is on the hearsay testimony of Joseph Sickert.

If Mary Kelly was the intended victim, it would explain why the killings ceased with her demise. However, surely any sinister organization capable of such a fiendish cover-up would have covered their tracks with more diligence? One also has to ask oneself why these purported criminal masterminds chose to disguise the killings as the frenzied work of a madman, when there would have been nothing easier than to make five prostitutes from the East End of London quietly disappear, with no questions asked. Instead the murders provoked a fever of panic, the like of which had never been witnessed before and which still has the capacity to arouse the most heated interest.

The proponents of the Masonic ripper theory get round this paradox by introducing Sir William Gull into the story. He first came to prominence in 1871 when he successfully treated the Prince of Wales for typhoid fever. To show her debt of gratitude, Queen Victoria raised him to the rank of baronet and bestowed on him the title Physician Extraordinary to the Queen. According to the conspiracy theory Gull, as the closest and most dependable servant of the Royal family, and a Freemason to boot, was asked to deal with the problem of the witnesses to the secret marriage.

However Stephen Knight is the only source of evidence that Gull was a Freemason and indeed the Masons have denied that he was admitted to the order. It has been suggested that Gull's meteoric rise to the most prominent medical position in the country was due to his influence as a Freemason but this is pure conjecture. In October 1887 Gull had a stroke and seemed to make a complete physical recovery although he was to suffer from aphasia, which caused hallucinations and seems to have effectively curtailed his career.

According to Knight, Gull was asked by the then Prime Minister Lord Salisbury, another Freemason, to deal with the problem of the blackmailers. However according to "The Freemason", 29 August 1903, Salisbury never joined the order.

An odd choice to cover up a scandal on which the future of the monarchy rested, Gull was supposedly driven round the streets of the East End by a coachman called John Nettley. The prostitutes were lured into the coach, stupefied with drugged grapes and then despatched, which would explain the lack of blood at the scene, which was remarked upon at the time. Catherine Eddowes' death is explained as a case of mistaken identity, because she had identified herself as Mary Kelly to the arresting officer.

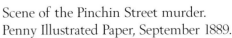

Scene of the Pinchin Street murder.
Penny Illustrated Paper, September 1889.

Lord Salisbury

Gull would go on to have two more strokes, the third of which would deprive him of speech and he was also over seventy years old at the time of the murders so is an unlikely candidate for roving the streets of the East End late at night. He suffers further indignity at the hands of Mr. Knight however who claims that not only did he operate on Annie Crook to remove her faculty for memory but his own death in 1890 was faked and in place of his body, a grave filled with stones was lowered into the family plot while he mouldered away in an asylum for another six years under the name Thomas Mason.

Knight's story falls apart under close scrutiny in other areas as well. For a start, rather than spending the rest of her life confined to an asylum, Annie Crook crops up quite regularly in various registers and records which can be verified at the Greater London Records Office. It would seem that Annie Crook inherited the condition of epilepsy from her mother, which was aggravated by alcoholism and poverty.

On January 22nd 1889 Annie and her daughter Alice, the cause of all the supposed fuss, were brought to Endell Street workhouse and left the next morning with no attempt being made to detain them. Eight years later, Annie's mother gives her daughter's address as the next of kin when she is taken to hospital with a head wound, no doubt caused by a fall during an epileptic fit. The address

is Drury Lane, and once again there is no indication that she has been taken against her will to an asylum or even that she is in hiding. Alice crops up again when she applies to St Pancras parish for work relief and does not seem to be making much of an effort to change her identity to escape the murderous designs of a plot hatched at the highest echelons of British society.

Records for the Hendon Infirmary show that she was suffering from hemiplegia, a partial paralysis of the body and she certainly spent the last thirteen years of her life in hospital. She was also diagnosed with spells of amentia, which is medically defined idiocy, but she was only transferred to the Lunacy Observation ward of the Workhouse four days before her death. Prior to this she was in Fulham Road Infirmary.

Furthermore, Annie Crook may not have been a Catholic in the first place. Alice was baptized a Protestant, and the entry records of the workhouses and infirmaries list her as such.

Another nail in the coffin for Knight's theory is that the Royal Marriages Act provided for just such a scenario. Instituted by King George III who wanted to prevent his sons making unsuitable alliances without his knowledge, it provided for the annulment of any royal marriage made without the king or queen's consent.

Catherine Eddowes' grave,
City of London Cemetery

Finally and perhaps most damning of all is the admission by Joseph Sickert, a self-confessed fantasist who had told a newspaper that the Yorkshire Ripper tried to kill him by running him over in his car. Two years after Knight's book was published he told the Sunday Times "It was a hoax; I made it up."

chapter 7

Any secret society is by nature shrouded in an aura of mystique and suspicion when viewed from the outside but Freemasonry has inspired such mistrust that it belongs almost in a league of its own. Every power base in history has sought to divert attention away from its own failings towards scapegoats and in Nazi Germany and Italy under Mussolini, hysteria was whipped up against the Freemasons.

What has changed over the years of course is that in Great Britain and the United States in particular, Freemasonry has been seen to have become that power base.

Medieval Masons observing the phases of the moon. They held lodge meetings during the week of the full moon.

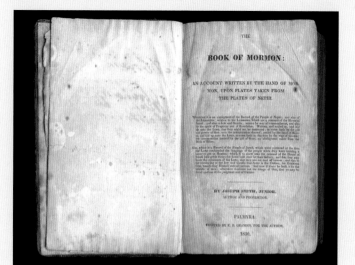

The Book of Mormon: An account written by the Hand of Mormon upon plates taken from the Plates of Nephi

The Dark

Hence, what started as a cloak of secrecy needed by freethinkers and intellectual radicals to protect them from persecution by the Church, has over the years been a victim of its success in becoming inextricably linked with the Establishment. Nowadays Freemasons are popularly considered to be the prime movers behind the façade of civilized society, the real force over and above the democratically elected parties, who will do anything to preserve the status quo that is so beneficial to them.

But this is not just a recent phenomenon. As early as 1826 rumors were spreading like wildfire of the malign influence that men bound to each other by clandestine blood oaths could have on the rest of society.

On March 13th of that year Captain William Morgan of Batavia, New York caused a sensation when he signed a book deal promising to reveal to the world for the first time the secrets of Freemasonry. In anger at his flouting the oath of secrecy, local Masons burnt the printer's shop and someone in power managed to get Morgan imprisoned for an outstanding debt. Although he was soon released, he was bundled into a coach on leaving the jail and never seen again.

In the investigation that followed, it was established that five Masons had taken him to the abandoned Fort Niagara but he had managed to escape and fled in the direction of Canada.

Naturally this story was implausible

Brigham Young led the great Mormon migration of 1846-48 and oversaw the church's establishment and growth in Utah

Joseph Smith

to a great many people and rumors proliferated that Morgan had been rowed out into the middle of a lake, weighed down with stones and pushed overboard.

At the subsequent trial it emerged that not only was the local sheriff a Mason, but so were the judge and most of the jury. But it did not stop there. The New York Governor DeWitt Clinton and the Secretary of State had also taken the blood oaths. This was a clear conflict of interest for elected officials whose first duty should have been towards the electorate and it seemed that the electoral process itself was seriously compromised.

Side

Feelings ran so high that there was sufficient weight of popular opinion to form a third political party, the Anti-Masonic Party, which was championed by John Quincy Adams who had been denied a second term by Andrew Jackson, a well-known Freemason.

In one of his many letters against Freemasonry he states,

"Cruel and inhuman punishments are equally abhorrent to the mild spirit of Christianity, and to the spirit of equal liberty. The infliction of them is expressly forbidden in the Bill of Rights of this Commonwealth, and yet thousands of her citizens have attested the name of God, to subject themselves to tortures, which cannibal savages would shrink from inflicting.

"It has therefore been in my opinion, ever since the disclosure of the Morgan-murder crimes, and of the Masonic oaths and penalties by which they were instigated, the indispensable duty of the Masonic Order in the United States either to dissolve itself or to discard forever from its constitution and laws all oaths, all penalties, all secrets, and as ridiculous appendages to them, all mysteries and pageants."

Despite the disappearance or murder of Morgan, the first expose of Freemasonry was published in 1827. As the century progressed, criticism of Freemasonry waxed and waned with the "cruel and inhuman punishments" and the usurpation of power, the main focus of censure.

In particular the ritual oaths attracted the attention of the Church. The Reverend C.G. Finney was so moved he wrote a book in which he condemns the Masonic lodge as a place "where men assembled to commit the utmost blasphemy of which they were capable, to mock and scoff at all that is sacred, and to beget among themselves the utmost contempt for every form of moral obligation."

He goes on to add that "these oaths sound as if the men who were taking and administering them were determined to annihilate their moral sense, and to render themselves incapable of making any moral discriminations, and certainly if they can see no sin in taking and administering such oaths under such penalties, they have succeeded, whether intentionally or not, in rendering themselves utterly blind, as regards the moral character of their conduct. By repeating their blasphemy they have put out their own eyes."

Not long after the Morgan affair the Freemasons were embroiled in another controversy, this time centered on the Mormons.

Joseph Smith, the founding father of the Mormons, finally settled in Nauvoo, Illinois with his followers after being hounded out of New York, Missouri and then Ohio. Freemasonry and Mormonism seemed to co-exist peacefully for a while, until the practice of polygamy crystallized an irreconcilable difference and became a source of increasing friction. Joseph Smith was ardently anti-Masonic as is evident in his supposedly divinely-inspired Book of Mormon. The suspension of five Mormon lodges by the Grand Lodge for "irregularities" only served to ratchet up the tension.

When a rift within the Church of the Latter-Day Saints prompted the printing of a pamphlet condemning Joseph Smith, he used his powers as mayor with the municipal council to have the printing press destroyed which provoked widespread rioting. The rioters could claim that the Mormons had suppressed the right to a free press enshrined in the Constitution. Smith responded by calling out the state militia to protect the city but he was promptly arrested for treason and incarcerated. On June 27th 1844, despite the pledge of protection of Governor Thomas Ford, a mob of men with blackened faces was able to storm Carthage jail and shoot Smith dead.

Smith's successor, Brigham Young was convinced that the Freemasons had engineered this chain of events and held them directly responsible for Smith's death. Such was his vehement conviction that he decreed any Mormon who henceforth had anything to do with Freemasonry would be excommunicated from the Church. For their part the Freemasons issued in essence the same decree to their members and it was not until 1984 that the two institutions were reconciled.

Since the first half of the nineteenth century two major scandals involving murder and conspiracies of silence have tainted the name of Freemasonry, namely the Whitechapel murders and the Banco Ambrosiano affair (see relevant chapters for details) and nowadays Freemasonry is much more likely to be associated in the public consciousness with an old boy's network which acts as a closed shop in business and

Isis, the Egyptian goddess of fertility, and her husband Osiris are linked to the origins of Freemasonry

public affairs, acting partially where a state of impartiality should exist.

This is a shame given the many charitable works that the Freemasons perform, and indeed in Stephen Knight's book "The Brotherhood: The Secret World of the Freemasons" many Masons are interviewed who deplore the way that the Craft has been abused by its own members.

One complaint made over and over again is that a point was reached when the membership of Freemasonry was dwindling so fast that the strict moral standards that would normally be applied to prospective initiates was dropped and gradually many lodges around the country (Great Britain) began to fill up with people who saw Freemasonry as a way to advance their careers and obtain unfair advantage in the business place. Essentially the purpose of Freemasonry for moral and psychological advancement had fallen by the wayside as the oath of brotherhood was used as a means to ensure a loyalty that could be called upon if the need arose.

One Detective Sergeant complained that

"I've seen Masonry used for rotten things in the force in recent years. I'd never have believed it was possible if I hadn't seen and heard it myself. What sickens me is the filthy distortion of the principles of Freemasonry. It's not meant to be for this, it's really not. But Masons are being promoted over the heads of non-Masons left, right and center. I've been to most of the police lodges in the City area and in the last few years it seems to me that the ritual and purpose of Masonry is getting less and less important. It's forbidden to talk about politics, religion or business in the Temple, but these yobbos (they shouldn't even be in the Police, let alone the Craft) they're using the secrecy to get into corners and decide who's next for promotion and who they can place where to their own advantage. Most of the time it's about how to protect themselves, but I've seen one or two things worse than that, actual criminal stuff. Nothing really terrible when you consider some of the things Old Bill Masons are supposed to have done here, but nevertheless I know people in the Craft who have had charges dropped as a result of little conferences at Lodge meetings."

Whereas once upon a time a Freemason might wait a considerable amount of time after he had been approached by a colleague or acquaintance to propose his membership, so that he could ensure he would bring something worthwhile to the Craft, some candidates were accepted after a matter of months before their character could properly be assessed.

It is also possible but by no means verifiable that Freemasonry was actively targeted by criminal elements who sought to abuse the oath of allegiance which would bind them to members of the justice and law

The inscription on Captain William Morgan's Monument, Batavia, New York. He was a Royal Arch Mason who wrote a book exposing the secrets of Freemasonry.

Dessiné par Mad.e la Marquise ⋆ ⋆ ⋆

1. Le Grand Maitre.
2. l'Orateur.
3. le Secretaire.
4.5.6. Freres aux Rouleaux
    de papier.

Assembleé de Francs-Maçons
Le Second Surveillant fait le signe
qui est pour lors en dehors
Dedié au très Galant, très sincere et très véridique Frere

Eighteenth century Masons
initiating a Master Mason, the
third and highest of the Three
Degrees of Freemasonry.
The approaching end of the
ritual of the initiate as he
passes from darkness to light,
is shown by the lit candles.

r la Reception des Maitres.

Maitre et va chercher le Recipiendaire

Loge avec le Frere Terrible.

e Leonard Gabanon Auteur du Catechisme des Francs-Maçons.

7. *le premier Surveillant.*

8. *le second Surveillant.*

9. *le Tresorier.*

10. *le Frere Sentinelle.*

Gravée par Mlle de J.

enforcement departments. A clear conflict of interests would thus prevail.

There have been cases of defendants making Masonic signs to a judge during a trial subsequent to which the due process of law was unquestionably thwarted. But conversely there was also one example when a judge stood down, telling the jury that he had just been given the Master Mason's Grand Hailing Sign of Distress by the defendant and his position of judicial arbiter was no longer tenable. In another instance a judge had actually given a defendant a harsher sentence when he was given a signal. When asked for his reasons he said that "the crime was more reprehensible because a Freemason had committed it, in spite of the moral teaching which Freemasonry entails and that the defendant had compounded his betrayal of Masonry by abusing the bond of brotherhood that existed between himself and the judge."

Most famously there was the case of Frederick Henry Seddon, accused of the murder by poisoning of his middle-aged lodger Eliza Barrow for financial gain.

On March 12th 1912 at the Old Bailey, when found guilty and given the chance to speak before the mandatory death sentence was passed, he made a Masonic sign to the Hon Mr Justice Bucknill, PC, also a Freemason and told him,

"I declare before the Great Architect of the Universe I am not guilty, my lord."

Those present in the court recall that the judge was visibly shaken. Here he was with no choice but to pass the death sentence on a defendant, whom, as a fellow Mason, he had sworn a blood oath to help.

When the judge recovered his composure he reminded the defendant of the charges and the overwhelming evidence against him which had led to the guilty charge.

"It does not affect me, I have a clear conscience" replied Seddon, remarkably calm.

"From what you have said, you and I know we both belong to one Brotherhood, and it is all the more painful to me to have to say what I am saying. But our Brotherhood does not encourage crime. On the contrary, it condemns it. I pray you again to make your peace with the Great Architect of the Universe."

This case is unusual in that the defendant made no attempt to pass a covert signal to the judge. By alerting the whole courtroom to the fact that there was an oath of brotherhood between himself and the judge he may have been trying to have the case ruled a mistrial but doing it at this late stage after the judge had summed up and the jury had returned with their verdict, there was only one direction in which the case could proceed.

Most attempts to influence a trial have been more subtle and have only been noted because of an otherwise inexplicable change in the judge's behavior. Now that most of the signals have passed into the sphere of public knowledge, an alert journalist or juror has occasionally spotted a non-verbal communication between judge and defendant but the documented instances are rare in the extreme and seem to belong to a bygone era when the influence of Freemasonry was far more prevalent than it is nowadays.

There have been occasions when police officers have made far clumsier attempts to signal their Masonic status by making a deliberate mistake in repeating the oath, "I swear by Almighty God..." substituting the "Great Architect" for "Almighty God" and then "apologizing" for their mistake.

Complaints have been made that this kind of allegiance is the most harmful because once a judge knows that an officer is a brother Mason he may not be as rigorous in ensuring that the proper procedures were followed to bring a suspect before the law, such as applying for search warrants and guaranteeing the rights of a detainee, all of which may prejudice a defendant's right to a fair trial.

Possibly the most injurious consequence of a common oath of brotherhood binding two sections of society together, which should at all costs be kept apart, is the fraternization of police officers and criminals.

In the 1970s Detective Chief Superintendent William Moody was sentenced to twelve years in prison and several other officers received lighter sentences for their part in a protection and bribery scandal run in conjunction with a group of racketeers and pornographers in Soho, London.

In the trial it became apparent that a corrupt network involving the officers and the criminals had formed in a Masonic lodge local to Moody.

The result of the publicity was a clean up of the Metropolitan Police which although successful was seriously hampered by the unwillingness of several officers to testify against fellow Masons.

Another way in which the principle of brotherhood vital to Freemasonry has been abused is in the promotion of Masons over their non-Masonic colleagues. It is important to make the distinction that it is the oath of allegiance rather than any inherent malignity of purpose within the doctrine of Freemasonry that is to blame.

As in the case of the judge who imposed a harsher sentence on a Mason for trying to sway his decision, there are undoubtedly many Masonic officers who find this use of the Craft abhorrent but as Stephen Knight's book "The Brotherhood" demonstrated, there are also those who would seek to gain unfair advantage by these underhand means.

There are many ways in which an officer seeking advancement might try to signal his Masonic status, that is if he were not already a member of the same lodge as his superiors. One method used in a written examination would be to make a slight downward indentation in the cross bar of a capital letter "A" so that it resembled the square and the compass, the Masonic Seal of Solomon.

At an interview, when a prospective candidate came to shake hands he could indicate which degree he had obtained to, by pressing his right thumb on the knuckle of the interviewer's index finger if he were an Entered Apprentice, pressing the second knuckle if a Fellow Craft and pressing between the knuckles of the middle and ring finger if a Master Mason.

Of course aside from any consideration of the corrupting influence this may have is the very high risk of not promoting the best person for the position and the attendant "brain drain" it could have on any organization, as disgruntled employees took their talents elsewhere.

Another sinister and wholly inappropriate use to which Freemasonry could be put by unscrupulous

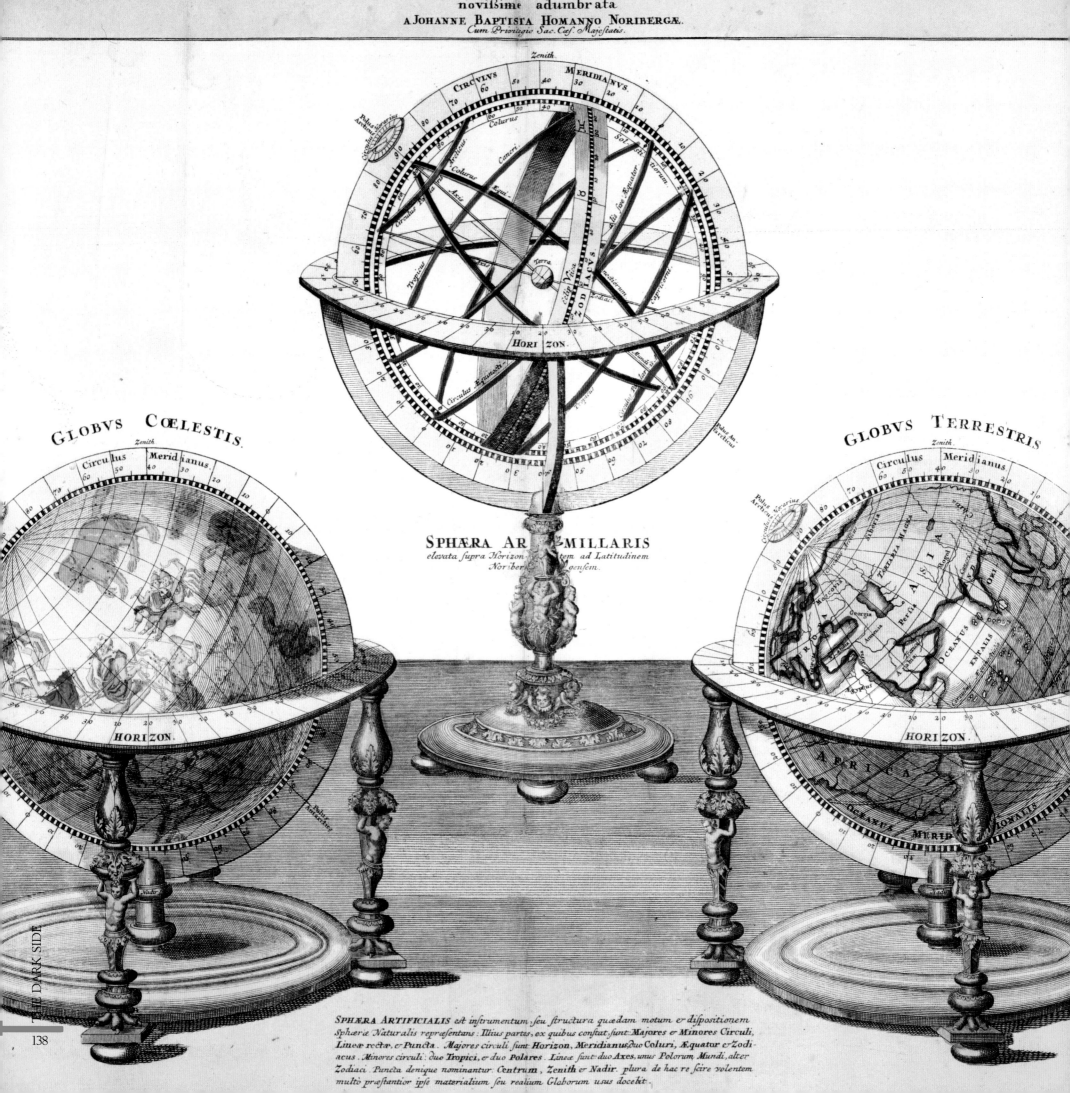

brethren, is the gathering and misuse of information. The wide range of men who had joined the ranks of the Freemasons, transcending class barriers and including men from all walks of life, many of them privy to sensitive information, such as magistrates, police officers, bank managers and solicitors, meant that as a potential resource for digging up dirt on people which could be used to blackmail or ruin someone, it was virtually unrivalled even by the official intelligence networks.

The worrying aspect of this is that an unsuspecting and altogether upstanding Freemason might pass on information to a fellow Mason who wanted it for his own devious ends, believing that the information was required for charitable purposes. After all, charity is one of the virtues held in highest regard by the Freemasons.

The huge number of solicitors involved in Freemasonry can apply their knowledge of the law to make matters very difficult for anyone who has incurred the wrath of a fellow brother. In one well-documented instance a partner of a law firm, who was not himself a Mason, blew the whistle on the corrupt practice of a Masonic partner, unaware that the firm was rife with Freemasons. He was promptly fired. When he asked another law firm to represent his claim for unfair dismissal, his former employers contacted the firm, the senior partners of whom were fellow Masons, and got them not only to drop the case but to act in their defence against any future claims on behalf of the former employee.

Not only can solicitors bring about financially damaging delays to court cases, in really corrupt cases they can actually be persuaded to mislead their own clients and run up enormous bills for useless paperwork and wasted man-hours. Compliant Freemasons in financial institutions can foreclose on loans and mortgages or withdraw credit.

After considering the potentially corrupting influence of Freemasons who choose to pervert the Masonic cause, let's turn to Freemasonry itself to examine the allegations regarding the blood oaths and rituals.

First of all, one thing that many people forget in a discussion of the oaths sworn in the name of secrecy, is that at no point does the initiate actually swear to carry out the punishment on a forsworn brother, rather he wishes the punishment on himself, and as such it should be read that to break the oath would be so heinous as to make the oathbreaker feel he deserved the worst punishment imaginable. And indeed it is hard to imagine a punishment worse than the ones described!

One of the most damaging accusations levelled at the Freemasons is that their rituals are tantamount to the black arts of devil worship and sorcery. The association of Freemasonry with Satanism has in no small part been crystallized in the public consciousness by the pronouncements of the Catholic Church, in particular the Papal Bull Humanum Genus promulgated by Pope Leo XIII, in which he goes so far as to use the words "kingdom of Satan."

Indeed Freemasonry itself must hold itself partly to blame for this misconception as its insistence on secrecy does a great deal to fan the flames of suspicion. The obsession with secrecy seems an outdated concept.

Globes played an important part in Masonic lodges in the early nineteenth century. They were always paired - one celestial and one terrestrial. The celestial globe symbolized the spiritual part of human nature while the terrestrial globe symbolized the material side.

It may once have had its uses when Masonic brethren might have faced persecution for their membership. If the Templar theory is correct, they would have faced not just persecution but the most horrendous bodily torture and mental degradation, followed by a slow roasting over hot coals.

There simply seems no need for it and indeed some prominent Freemasons have called for more transparency in their dealings because the covert nature of much of the activity has had the opposite effect to that originally intended and has served merely to invite bad publicity.

However it would seem that there are those within the ranks of Freemasonry who actually enjoy the cloak and dagger aspect and quite contrary to the explicit rules of Freemasonry not to discuss business or pervert its cause to further one's material ends, take every opportunity to exploit the clandestine network afforded by such a widespread brotherhood.

Nowadays the veil of secrecy has to all intents and purposes been lifted aside. After all, anyone interested enough to use a legal deposit library would have at his fingertips a whole host of literature on Freemasonry, some of which such as Richard Carlisle's "Manual of Freemasonry", describe the rituals in laborious detail. Lodges such as the United Grand Lodge in Great Queen Street in London have extensive libraries which are open to those interested in pursuing the subject yet there still exists this aura of secrecy, in the public's mind at least.

However it seems that Freemasons are damned if they do and damned if they don't for this very openness itself is taken as proof positive that there must be more

dark secrets that are kept back for those in the know and that the public has been spoon-fed a certain amount of harmless information both to satisfy its curiosity and take that curiosity down the wrong path.

There has grown up a conviction that most Freemasons themselves don't even know the real secrets of Freemasonry and only a select kernel, who have progressed right to the thirty-third degree, the inner sanctum of Freemasonry, are privy to the arcane lore that is at the heart of all the ritual and ceremony.

Certainly there has been much controversy over the nature of the Deity known as the Great Architect. One of most commendable things about Freemasonry is that its non-prescriptive attitude towards the nature of its members' faith has allowed a truly international and non-denominational brotherhood to develop. In a world increasingly divided along sectarian lines, which leads to shocking levels of violence and bloodshed, this is unique. The great power of Freemasonry to unite otherwise disparate and seemingly irreconcilable groups was perhaps nowhere better displayed that at the Royal Albert Hall in June 1967 when Arab and Israeli Masons joined in unison to celebrate the 250th anniversary just ten days after the Six Day War.

It was only made possible because the tenets of Freemasonry decree that so long as a man has faith in a "Supreme Being" he may be admitted to the brotherhood.

This principle was so fiercely adhered to, that when the Grand Lodge of Berlin announced in 1846 that they were henceforth refusing membership to non-Christians, the British Grand Lodges severed all ties with them until they reversed their decision. In fact so anxious was the Grand Lodge in Britain to extend the hand of brotherhood to the Hindus in India, that they argued that although to some eyes a pantheistic religion, the many gods of Hinduism were, when properly considered, all differing manifestations of one divine source.

However some writers have speculated that the "Supreme Being" which features so prominently in Masonic ritual and mythology is not a catch-all descriptive term to allow men of different faiths to come together but an actual deity in its own right.

This has obviously been extremely distressful to many Masonic brethren who suddenly found themselves questioning the compatibility of Freemasonry with their faith. This was not a problem for Roman Catholics for in Canon 2335 promulgated in 1917 it was decreed that "those [Catholics] who enrol in the Masonic sect or in other associations of the same sort which plot against the Church or the legitimate civil authorities" would be punished by "ipso facto excommunication."

But the Church of England in particular had a very high number of Freemasons in its ranks and the slightest hint of rituals designed to worship a non-Christian deity would have been of the gravest consequence.

The controversy centers around a name, which is revealed to a Master Mason on attaining to the Holy Royal Arch. Whether this is a side degree or an extension of the Third Degree, which completes the symbolic ordeal of the Master Mason, is disputed.

In his book "The Brotherhood" Mr. Knight advanced the contentious conclusion that the ineffable name of God, "JAHBULON" is not "a general umbrella term open to any interpretation an individual Freemason might choose, but a precise designation that describes a specific supernatural deity composed of three separate deities fused into one."

The theory is not a new one, for as long ago as 1873 the issue of the meaning of the word provoked the Masonic author and historian General Albert Pike, who later became Grand Commander of the Southern Jurisdiction of the Supreme Council of the 33rd Degree at Charleston, to write,

"No man or body of men can make me accept as a sacred word, as a symbol of the infinite and eternal Godhead, a mongrel word, in part composed of the name of an accursed and beastly heathen god, whose name has been for more than a thousand years an appellation of the Devil."

The theory is that Jahbulon is a tripartite word, each syllable representing a different deity.

Jah stands for Jawheh, or Jehovah, the God of the Hebrews, Bul for Baal, the fertility god of the Caananites, and On for Osiris, the Ancient Egyptian Lord of the Underworld.

The name that has caused the most upset of course is Baal, for over the centuries it has become inextricably linked with the Devil. In the sixteenth century, Baal was described as a devil with three heads, that of a man, a cat and a toad, atop the body of a spider.

However this use of the name is a medieval confection,

for it is originally a Hebrew word for "Lord". In the biblical story, in which Elijah challenges the unidentified deity called Baal to a competition with Jehovah, Baal ends up the ignominious loser and hence he is derisively labelled "Lord of the Flies" "Ba'al-zbub", which signifies that he is Lord of nothing at all. To medieval Christian scholars, the only rival deity that existed was the Devil and hence Beelzebub came to stand for Satan.

There is not even widespread agreement among Freemasons that the name "Jahbulon" refers to a triune Deity but of course the sensational story that the Freemasons worship some devilish Trinity with rituals steeped in black magic sells books and newspapers and more sober academic study goes limping after.

Some Freemasons have left the brotherhood because they cannot reconcile their Christian faith with Masonic principles and each time this happens it makes the headlines. What is often overlooked is that there are also millions of practising Christians who have no problems squaring their relevant commitments. They would no doubt take offence at the notion that they have somehow been hoodwinked by the upper echelons of Freemasonry into worshipping a false god, at the detriment to the divine source of their religion.

Ultimately of course there may be no definitive answer.

When "Darkness Visible" was written by Walton Hannah in 1952 it appeared to demonstrate conclusively that Christianity and Freemasonry were incompatible but then it was answered by an Anglican vicar in "Light Invisible: the Freemason's Answer to Darkness Visible"

and his arguments were equally plausible.

So on the one hand it was condemned because it was a,

"mystagogical system, which reminds us of the ancient heathen mystery-religions and cults, from which it descends and is their continuation and regeneration."

And on the other hand, it was lauded by an Anglican vicar, as,

"the oldest of all religious systems, dating from time immemorial. It is not in itself a separate religion, and has never claimed to be one, but it embodies in itself the fundamental truths and ancient mysteries on which every religion is based. Taunts that it worships a "common denominator" God are rather wide of the mark if the phrase indicates any inadequacy or limitation in nature or title of the God we worship, for we worship and believe as a first principle in the fullness of the Godhead of which other religions see only in part."

With this contradiction in mind let us examine the Masonic teachings that have caused so much controversy.

The cemetery of Pere-Lachaise, Paris, created by the French Mason Alexandre-Theodore Brongniart. Sphinxes, pyramids and obelisks featured in the design linking back to the Egyptian mysteries.

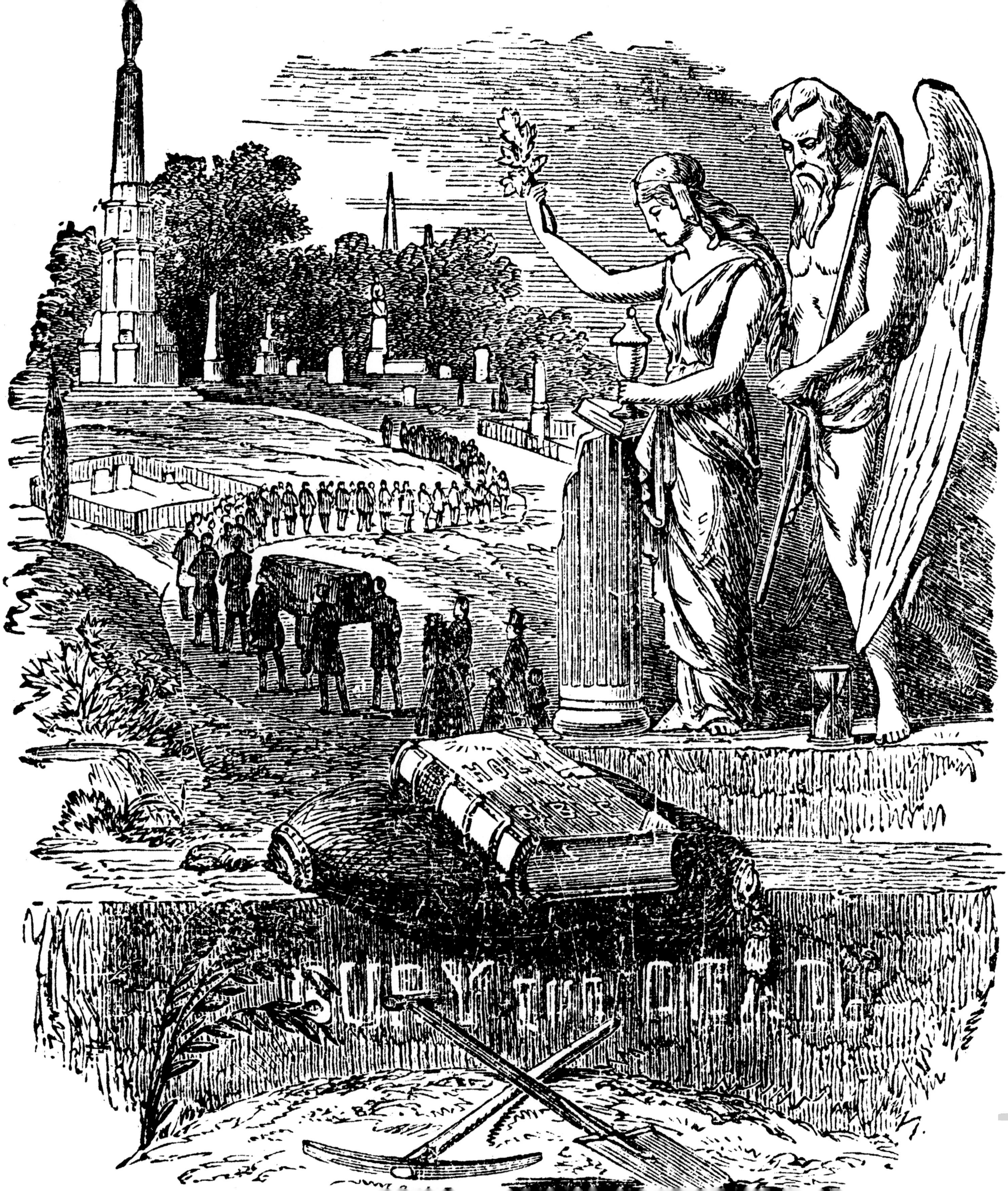

  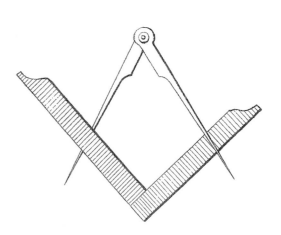

chapter 8

PERHAPS ONE OF THE MOST MISUNDERSTOOD ASPECTS OF FREEMASONRY IS IN ITS USE AS A DEVELOPMENTAL PSYCHOLOGY, USING SYMBOLS OF TRANSFORMATION, WHICH ARE ONLY "OCCULT" IN THE SENSE THAT THEY ARE NOT EASILY UNDERSTOOD BY THE UNINITIATED.

The beginnings of modern science were closely linked with those of Speculative Freemasonry. Seventeenth century illustration of an astrologer's costume

The Ark of the Covenant, containing the Ten Commandments, was housed within the Temple of Solomon

Speculative

As we have seen before, the allegory of the building of the Temple of Solomon is used to describe humanity as a whole and each Freemason must strive to improve himself to take his place as the perfect ashlar in the temple of humanity. However in Masonic ritual the temple is also used to describe the psyche. The Ground Floor might be equated with the individual consciousness, the Middle Chamber with the personal unconscious and the Holy of Holies with the collective unconscious as prefigured by the psychoanalyst Carl Gustav Jung.

Thus the progress of a Freemason through the three degrees becomes a journey of discovery and fulfilment of the Self and is a quest for enlightenment that takes a lifetime to achieve.

Entering into the Craft via the Ground Floor of Solomon's Temple, the candidate is still at a place in his life where his concerns are primarily with the material world and the physical side of life. He is made aware through the teachings of Freemasonry that if he is sufficiently honest and diligent in his undertaking he will be able to advance to a part of the Temple where he will be aware of the Deity, the divine source of existence which is left up to the individual to define according to the tenets of his chosen religion.

Psychoanalyst C.G. Jung

Thus the journey through the Temple may be considered in modern psychoanalytical terms as a journey into the unconscious. This is perhaps why Freemasonry has been deemed so secretive. The kind of insights available to someone who rigorously shines the light of truth down into the depths of their subconscious may be termed secret in that they are only available to someone who is prepared to undergo the sometimes painful soul-searching that is necessary.

A Masonic lodge may be considered the physical manifestation of whichever level of the candidate's psyche he is working on and the various symbols will help to focus the mind on the task in hand. Although these symbols may vary from lodge to lodge, and especially from country to country, there are three objects which will always be present. These are the Three Great Lights, the Volume of Sacred Law, the Square and the Compasses.

the sacred writings to symbolize the divine source of all things.

To help the initiate in the First Degree he is presented with a Tracing Board, which is a kind of visual aid, replete with Masonic symbolism to focus the mind on the work to be done at this level.

The tracing board shows the four levels of the lodge as follows:

Freemasonry

The Square represents the Psyche, the Compasses the Spirit and the Volume of Sacred Law the divine source from which they derive. The first two will be arranged in slightly differing ways in each degree to show the relation of the Psyche to the Spirit, but they will always rest on

The Ground Floor is represented by the Chequered Pavement, which consists of a mosaic of black and white squares. This is the level at which the material world operates.

The Middle Chamber, the level of the Psyche, is

Solomon builds the Temple.
The First Book of Kings, chapter 6, verses 11-14.

dominated by three columns, which we will examine in detail later.

The heavens, the region of the Spirit, is the Porchway entrance to the Temple and are depicted by the sun, the moon and the stars.

The final level is the very source of divinity itself and is represented by a blazing star, often referred to as the Glory, which occupies a prominent place right at the heart of the tracing board.

The aspiring Freemason learns, through lectures on the deeper meaning of the symbolism of the tracing board and application of that learning to his inner psychological processes, some fundamental truths about the nature of appearance and reality in the universe.

The black and white squares of the pavement teach him that although the universe often appears to be made up of seemingly opposing forces and principles, looking beyond the opposition to the floor as a whole reveals a pattern that has come together to create a harmonious whole. This is reinforced by the Tessellated Border, which runs along the edges of the Tracing Board, binding the picture together.

The position of the Glory points to a deeper understanding that the universe is but one single manifestation of the divine source. This is one of the first lessons that the initiate learns and it is known as the Law of Unity.

But this is only part of the picture for another abiding principle of Freemasonry is the Law of Duality, which is illustrated at the level of the Spirit by the complementary

nature of the sun and moon. On the one hand we have the meek and mild light of the moon which waxes and wanes, and on the other the burning bright light of the sun.

The level of the Psyche is dominated by three columns, which serve to further demonstrate the law of Duality. This Law states at both an individual and a cosmic level, that the moment something appears to exist in isolation from its divine source, the balance will be redressed by its polar opposite appearing as a complement.

The three columns also illustrate the Rule of Three. The Corinthian Column represents an active, creative, dynamic psychic energy, while the Doric Column represents a passive, pensive, reflective agency. The one expands, and the other contains and they must be kept in equilibrium by the third column for psychological and moral health to obtain. This third balancing column is the Ionic Column.

This association of psychical principles with architectural orders is descended from Vitruvius, the Roman architect and philosopher, who was among the first to incorporate dimensions of the human body into religious buildings. He taught that buildings used to worship warlike gods should follow the Doric Order, whereas those dedicated to the gods of sexual and romantic love should use the Corinthian Order.

Ascending from the level of the material world to the Glory is Jacob's Ladder. It will be noticed that around the outside of the Tracing Board the compass points have shifted 90 degrees anticlockwise so that East is at the

Carpenters at work making the Ark of the Covenant. Shittim, the Hebrew word for acacia, was revered in the Bible, as sacred wood from which the Ark of the Covenant was made.

top, and the Ladder leads in this direction towards the Blazing Star.

This brings to mind the catechism of the Entered Apprentice,

"From whence come you and whither are you travelling?"

"From the West, and travelling towards the East."

"Why do you leave the West and travel towards the East?"

"In search of Light."

To travel up the ladder is to move along the ascending dimensions of consciousness towards an awareness of the divine source of the universe. The position of the three Great Lights at the bottom of the ladder suggest that it is through the fundamental truths of Freemasonry that one will come to the realization of the divine spark within the human soul.

Beneath the Three Great Lights is the point-within-a-circle-bounded-by-two-parallel-lines. The parallel lines which are reminiscent of the two columns either side of the Temple gateway, Joachim and Boaz, can also be taken to represent the active and passive principles that must be kept in balance. In American Freemasonry they are equated with the rods of St. John the Baptist and St. John the Evangelist. In English Craft Masonry they represent Moses, the prophet

and Solomon the Law-giver.

Finally we note that the pathway to the Blazing Star is strewn with the symbols of Faith, Hope and Charity, which correspond to the three degrees of Craft Masonry. The Entered Apprentice who knows nothing of the road on which he has set out must trust to Faith. The Fellow Craft who can glimpse something of the light of truth ahead moves from Faith to Hope and the Master Mason who has travelled the road looks back towards his fellow brethren travelling the "Path of Honesty" and helps them to achieve their quest with acts of Charity.

Now let us examine the ritual for clues as to how the psychological development of the initiate is guided by his fellow brethren. When the idea is appreciated that the lodge is a model of the initiate's psyche, the instruction that the Inner Guard must be under the command of the Junior Warden starts to take on a symbolic significance for the Inner Guard represents the ego, one of seven levels of consciousness each in turn represented by an officer of the lodge.

The Junior Warden in turn stands for the Self. At first the initiate may be confused as to the distinction for he was living in a spiritual darkness which confuses the Self with the ego. Through the rituals and the

First, Second and Third Degree Tracing Boards. These Tracing Boards show all the symbols associated with Freemasonry. The Mosaic Pavement, the Square and Compass, the Pillars from King Solomon's Temple, the Skull and Crossbones, and the Stairway to Heaven.

lectures of Freemasonry and by paying close attention to his inner world, the Freemason will come to separate the two. Identification of the Self with the ego is a limiting and constraining existence, in which one is swayed by every impulse and stray thought, led hither and thither like a dog owner who cannot control the dog on the end of the lead. Once the ego is recognized for what it is and put in its proper role as subordinate to the Self, it leads to the first stirrings of an appreciation of one's will and the potential to control one's destiny.

To reach this state is to travel along the "Path of Honesty" for it requires much self-reflection and the refusal to turn away from sometimes unpalatable truths about oneself. The emergence of the Self is similar to many New Age traditions of meeting with one's spirit guide, a psychological manifestation, often represented by a wise old man, which seems to straddle the worlds of the Psyche and the Spirit.

However simply repeating the rituals and going through the motions is not enough. An initiate is enjoined to make a daily advance in his Masonic knowledge and by this it is understood that he will carry away the principles into his daily life and watch for the process of psychological change, initiated within the lodge to pervade the other spheres of his life.

It is expected that if he perseveres in his quest he will experience a moment of profound psychological and spiritual insight. This is the real beginning of his path through the three degrees of Craft Masonry and in allegorical terms represents the moment when he leaves the bedrock of society and becomes the rough ashlar

which will be shaped to take its place within the Temple walls.

He will no longer be part of the amorphous mass of humanity which drifts through life, swept this way and that by the tides of fate. Rather he will become an individual responsible for his own destiny, armed with the sword of truth to forge his own destiny. With this new found power will come the duty to act responsibly with regard not just to his fellow brethren but to all mankind.

From this moment onwards, he will never be the same again for his experience cannot be "unexperienced" and therefore the decision to become a Freemason must not be entered into lightly. To help him deal with his new-found level of existence, he will need the Working Tools of the Entered Apprentice. These are tools of action,

The baptism of Jesus. The Gospel according to St. Matthew, chapter 3, verses 13-17.

which deal with a physical existence and the psychological capacities related to living in the material world, which is the preoccupation of the Ground Floor.

The Gavel represents active force, passion, energy and exuberance. By contrast the Chisel is a passive instrument in that it receives the blows of the Gavel and gives them precision and direction. As such it can be likened to the capacity for rational, analytical thought.

The 24-inch Gauge represents measured choice, and is once again a tool of balance, in that the Freemason must henceforth be mindful to fit the appropriate psychological capacity to the task in hand. The Gauge in this sense can be taken to direct the candidate to the need not only to identify the psychological capacities for passion and analysis within himself but to bring them under conscious control, and hence see them as tools which are there for him to use, rather than compulsive behaviors beyond his control.

This association of one's emotional and intellectual processes with tools separate and distinct from the personality brings with it a great sense of freedom from the tyranny of being pulled this way and that by psychological impulses which seemed to dominate the personality to such an extent that they seemed in fact to be the personality. With this freedom comes a sense of power, and of course with power comes the inherent potential for abuse of that power. This is why the initiate is urged to examine his conscience and the workings of his unconscious with which task the Second Degree of Freemasonry will equip him with the appropriate tools.

The Entered Apprentice who has undergone the psychological transformation necessary to complete the First Degree may feel he has already come a long way but he is only a third of the way through his journey and he has much serious work still to be done.

So far he has only taken control of the lowest level of his Psyche, the Ground Floor, and now he must continue

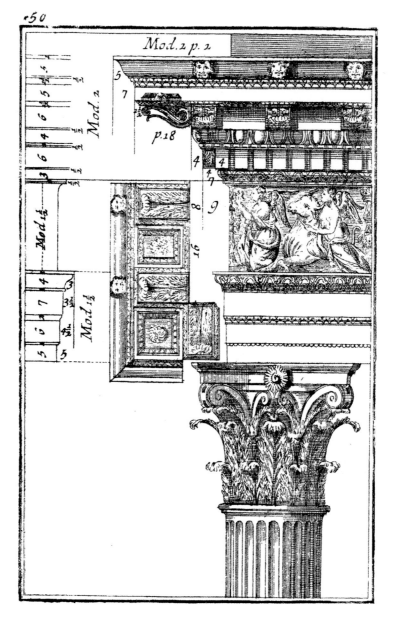

According to Masonic tradition, classical architecture derived
its most important principles from King Solomon's Temple

the interior quest if he is to travel along the dimensions of consciousness from the West to the East.

Now the Entered Apprentice reaches the area of the Temple of Solomon known as the Middle Chamber.

Here the significance of the point within the circle bounded by two parallel lines becomes apparent. Just as the First Degree Tracing Board represented man within the material plane, the Second Degree Tracing Board shows the psychological interior of man. Jacob's Ladder, which showed the way man could advance from an appreciation of the symbol of the Divinity, the Volume of sacred Law, to direct experience of the Deity itself, represented by the Glory or Blazing Star, is here shown as a winding interior staircase.

Either side of the staircase stand two pillars, which recall the Doric and Corinthian columns of the First Degree. They also bring to mind the Pillars of Cloud and Fire in the Book of Exodus and represent the complementary active and passive principles.

The lecture of the Second Degree reminds the Fellow Craft that these two columns are made of brass and cast in the clay ground. As such they are grounded in the material world, despite the celestial globes which are affixed on top. They are also hollow to store the archives of Freemasonry safe from flood or fire. With a little leap of the imagination we can see that the archival records relate to memories stored in the personal unconscious. Hitherto unavailable for reference, they are now a rich source for self-reflection on the part of the Fellow Craft.

The prominent position flanking the staircase through which he must enter on his journey along the Pathway of Honesty indicates that he must pass through or beyond them i.e. he must rise above their influence if he is to ascend the ladder. Memories make up a significant portion of what we understand as the personality and their power is such that they can both compel us towards certain behavior and constrain us, hence the duality of the symbol of the pillars.

As such they can have an unwarranted power over the choices we make and the subsequent direction in which this takes us. Often these memories were formed at a very early age and the lessons they brought with them are quite unsuitable for a mature individual. Part of the process of taking responsibility for one's life is examining these memories and rising above them, that is to say acknowledging their importance but refusing to let them hold sway over the course of one's life.

This kind of soul-searching, whereby deeply repressed memories are brought to the surface so that their emotional charge can be released, is hard and painful work. It is something that with modern psychoanalytical methods would be done in the company of a skilled and understanding professional. In Freemasonry, one's fellow brethren take the place of a therapist and hence we begin to appreciate the strong ties of brotherhood which are so inherent in the Craft.

In keeping with the Rule of Three there are three tools to help the Mason in his journey into the Middle Chamber of the Temple. Of course freeing oneself from the constraints of a learnt and sometimes arbitrary morality is only part of the story, for once these standards have disappeared the Fellow Craft finds that Free Will is

1. Le Grand Maitre.
2. l'Orateur.
3. le Recipiendaire.
4. le Secretaire.

Assemblée de Francs-Maçons,

Le Recipiendaire fait serment, a

de ne jamais reveler

Dedié au très Galant, très sincere et très véridique Frere

la Reception des Apprentifs.

...précation la main sur l'Evangile

...teres de la Maçonnerie.

...eonard Gabanon, Auteur du Catechisme des Francs-Maçons.

5. Le p.r Surveillant.
6. le 2.e Surveillant.
7. le Tresorier.

Masons assemble to initiate an Entered Apprentice. In this eighteenth century illustration, the Master of the Lodge is questioning the candidate before he reveals the secrets of the First Degree to him.

There are two distinct meanings given
for the letter G: Geometry and God

a loaded gift. Without an ethical lodestar he finds himself
adrift in a moral vacuum.

In some versions of Freemasonry this is likened to the
Fall of Lucifer from Grace as there is a chance that the
Fellow Craft will be consumed with pride at the power
he has achieved over himself and may choose to rebel
against the divine principle inside him and "fall" whether
gradually or suddenly into a materialistic and dissipated
existence. An example of this may be someone who from
an early age has had his natural impulses constrained by
his parents and has led a life of restraint and sobriety.
Finding himself freed from a life of forced behavior he
may choose to revel in the side of life he feels was closed
to him against his will.

This is where the tools of the Fellow Craft come
in. The Square, the Level and the Plumb-Rule are tools
of testing, they are methods of testing one's actions
against standards of morality. With the disappearance
of the conventional morality of his upbringing, held in
balance between the constraints of the ego and superego
as represented by the two pillars, the Freemason may
wonder where to turn for this new criterion against
which he must judge his actions. Hence the importance
of the Volume of Sacred Law, for Freemasonry recognizes
that the scriptures of all the monotheistic religions are
essentially the revealed truth of an internal relationship
between the psyche and its divine source which come
into contact at the realm of the Spirit.

The Plumb-line and the Level measure against the
vertical and horizontal planes, both of which, in order
to have any meaning, must have an absolute rather than

a relative value. In Masonic lore the Level represents judgement and the Plum-rule represents mercy. The Square of Truth maintains the balance necessary for internal psychological good health, which in simple terms could be defined as not being too hard on oneself but not going too soft either.

The second of the Three Immovable Jewels, the perfect ashlar, is the stone on which the Fellow Craft must test his new tools. It would be a mistake for him to consider himself the perfect ashlar at this stage. Rather the perfect ashlar is there as a reminder of the absolute moral law that exists within him. In the absence of the conventional morality that he has abandoned, the perfect ashlar is something against which he can judge his actions.

At this point the maturing Fellow Craft is represented as a ripening ear of corn, however he has only proceeded so far in his journey and his "education" is incomplete. There is always the possibility of abusing the new found wisdom and power which comes from the control over one's destiny gained in the Second Degree. This is why the subject of Wages is introduced at this point.

During the building of Solomon's Temple, the Fellow Craft Freemasons went "without scruple or diffidence" to the Middle Chamber to collect their wages, because of the confidence they placed both in themselves and in their paymasters. The

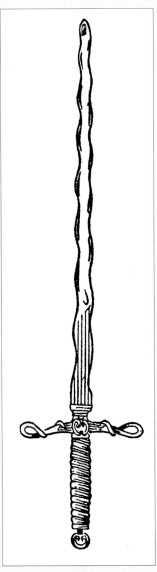

Fellow Craft is thus guided to the understanding that one's wages are one's just desserts. As St. Paul would have said, "As ye sow, so shall ye reap" but this is not divine providence rather it is similar to the process of karma worked out at the level of the soul, for that is what the Middle Chamber represents.

The reliance that the Temple builders placed in their paymaster suggests that the paymaster is honest and fair and so one should look to oneself rather than to external agencies, for the responsibility of one's fate. So the blessing of freedom of choice comes with a warning to the Fellow Craft. The acceptance of the burden of one's fate is daunting but incredibly empowering and means that one will never again blame others for one's own problems, thus allowing a true sense of forgiveness to emerge in those who might otherwise have harbored feelings of resentment.

The presence of the All-seeing Eye or in some cases the letter G, signifying the initial of the Deity, indicates that one's actions are observed in that they have consequences, both for oneself and others. In this respect it may symbolize one's conscience, which must be squared with one's actions. It also shows that the blazing star which could only be reached at the top of Jacob's Ladder in the Tracing Board of the First Degree can be seen within the Middle Chamber, or the level of the soul and this gives the Fellow Craft hope,

The Tyler's sword was wavy in shape, alluding to the "sword which was placed at the east of the Garden of Eden, which turned every way to keep the way of the Tree of life"

who as an Entered Apprentice, had to operate solely on faith.

As in the First Degree the interior winding stair ascends towards the Deity from the West to the East through seven dimensions of consciousness which advance the Fellow Craft from a connection to the material world to a point where he is able to apprehend the divine source of all things.

The seven dimensions are represented by seven officers of the lodge, which is in itself a physical manifestation of the Psyche. Each officer in turn is associated with a body of classical and renaissance literature illustrating the seven liberal arts and sciences, which the Fellow Craft is advised to study diligently.

The Tyler who stands guard outside the lodge represents Grammar, which enables the world of ideas to crystallize in the physical world of speech and debate. The Tyler could also be said to occupy the point at which the psyche reacts with the physical world, filtering information and protecting the psyche from unwelcome and overwhelming intrusion.

The Inner Guard as we have already seen stands for the ego, the psychological capacity with which we relate to the outside world. It is associated with Logic, which lays down the rules for analysis and rational thought.

The Junior Guard operates at a level of feeling and emotion and is bound to the liberal art of Rhetoric which appeals to the conscience of the listener. It also relates to memories stored in the unconscious and the ability to move across the threshold of consciousness to retrieve those memories.

The Senior Deacon operates at the level of Awakening, which implies a growing awareness of one's real nature. He is also associated with the Science of Arithmetic, used to give form to abstract ideas.

The Junior Warden is akin to our modern concept of the Self as described by Jung, which emerges into consciousness during a Freemason's advancement through the initial stages of the Craft. He is twinned with Geometry: "a science whereby we find out the contents of bodies unmeasured by comparing them with those already measured."

The Senior Warden represents the dimension of consciousness known as the Soul and is associated with Music which was considered a science by Renaissance and Classical scholars, not an art. As such it is concerned with harmony, both on an internal psychological level and at a celestial level.

The Worshipful Master is in contact with the Spirit in the same way that the Tyler was in contact with the physical world. At this level of consciousness the divine source can be perceived and that is why he is associated with the Science of Astronomy which is concerned with mapping the heavens and charting the movements of the celestial spheres, which in renaissance times were thought to directly influence human affairs. One might liken this to the principle, "as above, so below."

Climbing the winding staircase through the seven dimensions of consciousness is the aim of the Freemason but at this stage of the Second Degree, the Fellow Craft still has the hardest part of his journey ahead of him.

Once he has found the power within to exercise his

will freely in accordance with the absolute standard of morality that resides within his soul he finds he must surrender his will to a higher authority if he is to proceed to the level of a mature Master Mason.

Much progress has been made thus far. As an Entered Apprentice, the First Degree taught him that although he was a physical being living in a material world, this was not the whole story. The Second Degree taught him that rather than a physical being he was in fact a psychological being, occupying a physical shell. To advance beyond this concept of himself, he will have to "die" to this idea and be reborn to the realization that he is in fact a spiritual being, occupying both a psyche and a body.

So far the Fellow Craft's experience of his existence is defined by the limits of the Self. To progress beyond this existential boundary, the death of the Self must be sought and this is what the ritual drama of the third degree accomplishes. The Fellow Craft may be considered to be the Temple of Solomon, which is near to completion. The Temple cannot be finished because this psychological structure which he has been working on is incomplete.

To progress to the realm of the Spirit entails a psychological death of the mature Fellow Craft, which is symbolically enacted through the story of the murder of Hiram Abiff, the architect of the Temple. We are told that the secrets of a Master Mason were lost as a result of the murder because they could only be revealed when all three Grand Masters were present, that is to say, King Solomon, the King of Tyre and Hiram Abiff.

"This last and greatest trial by which alone he can be admitted to the secrets of the Master Mason's Degree" is not to be undertaken lightly but he who has undergone the rigours of the preceding degrees has a right to demand it, indeed he can progress no further with the knowledge and level of self-understanding he has so far attained.

According to the tenets of Freemasonry, when the time is right, the Deity will engineer the "ordinary duties of one's station in life" to facilitate the attaining of a new level of awareness. This is why the Masonic brethren are always enjoined to pay close attention to the daily events of their lives. Freemasonry is not something to be contemplated secluded from the outside world, rather it

Adam and Eve after the expulsion,
Genesis, chapter 3, verses 17-21

should be wrapped up in every waking moment of one's life, lived and experienced in the real sense of the world rather than merely contemplated.

He will find himself in a situation, which he thinks he is admirably equipped to deal with. Imagine his shock therefore on finding that his capacities for analysis and action fall hopelessly short. He feels betrayed, helplessly confused as to why his hitherto well-honed capabilities are failing him. He is aware of a means of avoidance and self-preservation but his moral standard is too well calibrated by this time to allow him to make use of it and so he turns to the East, to the source of divinity to which he has orientated himself in times of need but rather than helping him, it kills him and he finds himself buried in the rubble of the Temple which he has been building so assiduously

What has in fact died is his concept of himself as a soul, which is just as much of an illusion as his concept of himself as a physical being. Just at the point of his utmost despair, the Worshipful Master, bringing with him a consciousness of the Spirit, enters the Psyche with the life-giving realization that he is a Spiritual being with a soul and a body. This awareness lifts the initiate from the "grave" and he finds himself in the Porchway Entrance to the Holy of Holies, through which he is able to glimpse the Deity, the source of his divine spirit and suddenly his problems seem to

disappear, his eyes have at last been opened.

There is however another sense in which the ritual of the "death" can be understood, which takes us back to an allegorical interpretation of Genesis. Many gnostic sects, and there are cogent arguments for believing that Freemasonry is a modern school of gnosticism, read the creation story of Adam and Eve in a symbolic way and indeed laughed at early Christians who took a literal interpretation of the story of Genesis.

In December 1945 Muhammad, Khalifa, and Abu al-Majd were digging for sabakh, or bird-lime, with four camel-drivers near their home in al-Qasr, six kilometers from the town of Nag Hammadi. Muhammad's spade hit a large earthenware jar buried beneath the sand and inside were rolls of parchment, which had been buried in the sand sometime in the fourth century. Known nowadays as the Gnostic Gospels these texts shed new light on early Christian sects who took a very different view on the teachings of Christ to that which has been handed down to us as orthodoxy.

One of these texts called the Exegesis of the Soul takes a similar reading of Genesis to the one implied in the Masonic interpretation of the myth of the fall of mankind. Adam represents the Consciousness and Eve represents the Psyche. In the beginning there was a primordial being, called Adam, from whom God took

The Gnostic Gospels shed new
light on early Christian sects

one side and created Eve, which represents the projection of the Psyche from Consciousness. However the Psyche leads Consciousness into identification with the body, which is symbolized by the expulsion from Eden.

The Exegesis of the Soul also draws on Homer's The Iliad and the Odyssey, in which Helen has been abducted and has to be rescued. In these tales Helen represents the Psyche, and her abduction symbolizes the fall of the Psyche into incarnation. Plato's Phaedo in which he narrates the discussion that took place between Socrates and his friends during the last hour of his life, concerning the immortality of the soul, illustrates this fall and redemption of the Psyche.

"The Psyche is dragged by the body into the region of the changeable, where she wanders in confusion. The world spins around her and she is like a drunkard under its influence. But returning to herself, she reflects. Then she passes into the realm of purity, eternity, immortality and the unchangeable, which are her kindred. When she is herself and not obstructed or hindered she is ever with them. When she ceases from her erring ways and is in communion with the unchanging, she is herself unchanging. This state of the Psyche is called Sophia."

The myth of Persephone and Demeter, which was so central to the classical mystery schools practicing the Eleusinian rites is another allegory of the descent of Psyche into incarnation. Persephone represents the fallen psyche

and Demeter, her mother, stands for the pure psyche in its pristine condition. In the myth, Hades abducts Persephone and takes her to the Underworld. Her mother wanders the earth searching for her and learns from the sun god Helios that Zeus had conspired with Hades to lure Persephone away from her mother so that she could be captured. In her wrath, Demeter renounces the gods and wanders the earth disguised as an old woman.

She eventually comes to rest in Eleusis where she would sit grieving in the shade of an olive tree by the Maiden's Well. Here her sorrow grew as she watched the king's daughters laughing as they drew water and in her grief she dropped a strand of her grey hair into the well and poisoned the water, which had nourished the growing corn.

From then on, the land was barren and nothing would grow, and the golden fields of corn withered and died. Mankind reaching the point of near starvation, reverting to cannibalism and savagery. Seeing all the good work of the gods undone, Zeus commanded Hades to release Persephone and sent Hermes to fetch her. Hades however gave Persephone a pomegranate seed to eat, which meant that she had to return annually to the Underworld for a third of the year. Demeter's joy at being reunited with her daughter was such that she immediately revoked her spell which had plagued the land and once again the golden ears of corn were flourishing in the soil. In recompense she shared

The widow's son is known to members
of the Fraternity as Hiram Abiff

with the princes of Eleusis her sacred rites and mysteries which enabled men to rise from the grave to the bright sunshine of the fields of Elysium, the abode of the blessed in the afterlife, in the same way the seeds of corn emerged from the soil.

Hades abducting Persephone into the Underworld

Taken on one level, this story could be read as an attempt by the classical mind to grasp the wonders of mother nature which seem to disappear for so long only to return as if from the dead to light up the fields and hedgerows with the sights, sounds and smells of Spring. However it should be read on a rather more sophisticated level as an attempt to square the spiritual flame which flickers in man's soul with the brute nature of his physical existence. The grief felt by Demeter represents "metanoia" or the grief felt by Psyche at the separation from her true nature, when she is incarnated into the material world. When Hermes rescues Persephone and returns her to her mother we should read this as a rescue of the Psyche from the spiritual darkness, which exists when she identifies herself with the circumference of the circle of the Self. Her true nature is the point at the center and reuniting them is a spiritual reawakening, which brings a surge of joy as is noticeable in the air when spring returns and winter is banished.

Remember the prominence given to the symbol of the point-within-a-circle as representing the initiate in Craft Masonry and the

comparison of the Fellow Craft to a ripening ear of corn.

The pomegranate seeds are the seeds of future lives which we create by our actions in the present life, which result in our reincarnation until the journey of awakening is complete. We call this karma without really understanding what is involved. The ancients would have called it "fate." The significance of the third of the year is a reference to the threefold nature of the Self: Consciousness, Psyche and the Physical Body.

With this frame of reference let us now return to the book of Genesis and consider the mystical interpretation that was so central to certain gnostic Christian schools. In such a reading the act of creation would refer not to the physical universe but the world of the Spirit and the world of the Psyche. Thus the fall of Adam wherein he is expelled from the Garden of Eden represents the incarnation of the human spirit, which meant that it could no longer "walk with God", which is to be understood as a loss of direct communion with God.

According to this theory, before birth, we have a Spirit, a Soul and a Self and when we incarnate or are conceived, we receive our physical shell. The moment of conception removes us from a blissful state of innocence in which we are in intimate contact with the Deity.

Referring back to the ritual

Left: In Freemasonry, the Sun and Moon together represent wisdom, power and goodness. The study of the "stellar world" is an important feature of Freemasonry

The ruins of classical civilization fascinated Rennaissance scholars

murder of Hiram Abiff we can say that his death represents the moment when the Self is overwhelmed by its confinement in the material plane and loses consciousness of its contact with its Soul, Spirit and divine source. It is only possible to return to the pre-lapsarian state of bliss when the three principal officers (the Self, the Soul and the Spirit) are reunited but until then the initiate as Hiram Abiff is buried in a symbolic grave whose dimensions give a clue as to the restrictions a physical and psychological life without the spiritual entail.

It is "three feet east and three feet west" suggesting that the dimension of consciousness is curtailed. It is also "three feet between north and south" suggesting a limitation on the capacity for action and restraint and it is "five feet or more in depth" which makes one think of the height of a body, the physical shell in which he is trapped. Just like the tracing boards of the first two degrees, the Tracing Board of the Third Degree represents the human individual, this time in the form of a coffin, which leads to the conclusion that ignorance of the spiritual side of existence is akin to death. Dying to this concept of the Self is actually rebirth and is the only way to realize our full human potential.

If you look carefully you will notice that the compass points have reoriented so that at the top is the West and East is at the bottom. This should be taken to mean that the Master Mason having reached this new level of spiritual awareness no longer yearns for the light of truth in the East for he has already arrived there. Now he turns back to look in the direction he has come towards his fellow brethren who are themselves setting out on their own journeys along the Path of Honesty.

No longer reliant on the virtues of Faith or Hope, he now embodies Charity as he helps his brethren to achieve what he has achieved. In the Tracing Board of the First Degree, Charity is pictured on the highest rung of Jacob's Ladder, encompassing the three planes, with her feet in the material world, her body in the world of the Psyche and her head in the world of the Spirit, bathed in the glow which emanates from the Blazing Star.

To help him in his new role as Master Mason and the responsibilities to his fellow brethren that this position entails he is endowed with three tools. Unlike the tools of the previous two degrees, which were tools of action and testing, these are tools of creativity. In architectural terms they could be seen as tools of planning and design, the Pencil, the Skirrett and the Set of Compasses.

The Pencil represents the place in the unconscious, which is touched by the Spirit and results in creativity. It could be called inspiration and the tip of the Pencil, which is the point at which material from the Psyche, one's thoughts, manifest themselves in the physical world, represents the interface between the psychological and the spiritual worlds.

Of course endless revelation and creativity would simply overwhelm the Psyche and that is where the Skirrett comes in. It is a tool, which sets limits on the application of the Pencil, and in a psychological sense it represents the use of fundamental principles without which creativity is comparable to madness. The one without the other is creatively sterile in a practical sense and hence they need conscious balance. Hence the Compasses, an instrument which assigns proportion in geometrical terms and in a psychological sense assures a steady flow from the revelatory source of spirit bounded by a set of principles to assure psychic good health.

Once again the level of advancement attained in the Third Degree is represented by one of the three Immovable Jewels which in this case is the Tracing Board itself. This serves to remind us that this degree is concerned not with the individual stones of the Temple, but with the relationship between them which could be found on the Principal Architect's drawing board. Thus the Master Mason is reminded of his duty to those who perhaps have not yet found their proper place within the structure of the Temple and need his help.

The level of consciousness which he now commands can be ascertained by examining where the lodge of the Master Masons is supposed to convene. This is called the Porchway Entrance to the Holy of Holies, which is illuminated by the light of the Divinity, which shines through the symbolic Dormer Window. Beneath their feet lies the same black and white chequered floor, which was a symbol of duality in the First Degree.

The Entered Apprentice was uniquely concerned with his relationship to the material world and saw the black and white squares as symbols of opposition and differentiation.

The Master Mason has come to a spiritual understanding of himself and his place in the physical plane and in the light which emanates from the Dormer Window he can

see that even the seemingly polar opposites of the black and white are in fact all just the play of shadow and light which come from the same divine source.

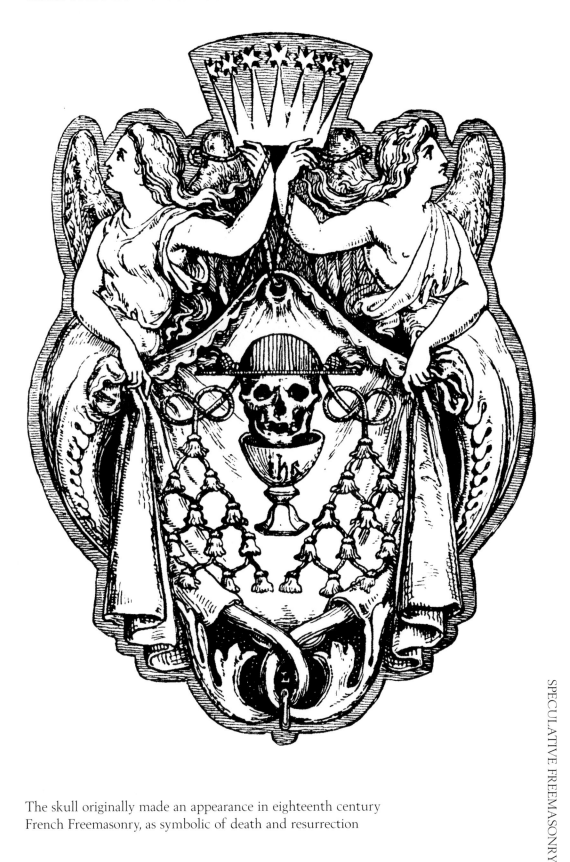

The skull originally made an appearance in eighteenth century French Freemasonry, as symbolic of death and resurrection

chapter 9

SYMBOLISM IS VERY IMPORTANT TO FREEMASONRY. IN A PRE-LITERATE AGE, SYMBOLS WERE USED AS TEACHING TOOLS, BOTH TO CONVEY MEANING AND CARRY INFORMATION. AFTER ALL, IMAGES MAKE A MORE LASTING IMPRESSION ON THE MIND THAN WORDS DO. THEY CAN ALSO HIDE MEANING FROM THE UNINITIATED AND THEREFORE THEY WERE A USEFUL WAY TO IDENTIFY ONESELF WHEN IT WAS DANGEROUS TO BE A FREEMASON.

BECAUSE OF SPECULATIVE FREEMASONRY'S BACKGROUND IN STONE MASONRY, MASONIC SYMBOLS ARE OFTEN TO BE FOUND CARVED IN THE MOST UNLIKELY PLACES IF YOU KNOW WHAT TO LOOK FOR, AND MANY OF THE MOST FAMOUS BUILDINGS IN HISTORY ARE WOVEN INTO THE MYTHS OF THE ORIGINS OF THE CRAFT.

The Knights Templar were a monastic military order and within two centuries had become rich and powerful enough to defy all but the Pope in Rome

The Apprentice's Pillar in Rosslyn Chapel. Legend has it that the apprentice was killed by the Master Mason, consumed with envy at the beauty of the workmanship.

Masonic

ROSSLYN CHAPEL

Perhaps nowhere is the connection between the Knights Templar and the Freemasons better illustrated than at the chapel south of Edinburgh built by William St. Clair in 1440 known as Rosslyn Chapel. It is a veritable treasure-trove of enigmatic ciphers encoded into the ornate architecture and has attracted seekers after the Holy Grail from all over the world convinced that the Templars brought back the Grail from the Holy Land and hid it in an underground vault beneath the chapel.

Dan Brown has contributed much to the mystical atmosphere of the place, using the chapel as one of the scenes in his "The Da Vinci Code."

He describes it thus:

"Every surface of the chapel had been carved with symbols − Christian cruciforms, Jewish stars, Masonic seals, Templar crosses, cornucopias, pyramids, astrological signs, plants, vegetables, pentacles and roses. The Knights Templar had been master stonemasons erecting Templar churches all over Europe but

Rosslyn was considered their most sublime labor of love and veneration. The Master Masons had left no stone uncarved. Rosslyn Chapel was a shrine to all faiths... to all traditions... and, above all, to nature and the goddess."

His claim that the chapel was built by the Templars is however somewhat fanciful as they had been suppressed as an order at the beginning of the fourteenth century but it is just possible that they went underground and survived as a secret society.

Supposedly the chapel was built as an exact replica of the Temple of Solomon, with a west wall, a rectangular sanctuary and a Holy of Holies. Interestingly one of the carvings is said to depict a Freemason undergoing the ritual of initiation before a gure dressed as a Templar.

The Chapel also contains a pair of columns that are supposed to represent the pillars that stood outside the Temple.

Architecture

Rosslyn Chapel is said to be modelled on Herod's Temple

JOACHIN AND BOAZ

Joachin (or Jachin, the spelling varies) stood on the right of the Temple entrance and Boaz on the left. According to Masonic legend they symbolized the power of the Supreme Being. The Hebrew translation of Jachin is "for God will establish" and the translation of Boaz is "strength in him."

The names no doubt refer to the carvings that adorned them: "May the Lord establish the throne of David and his kingdom for his seed forever" and "In the strength of the Lord shall the King rejoice."

These two pillars are themselves said to be copies of two even older pillars, which according to Masonic lore were built by the children of Lamech. They carved their compendium of knowledge of the Arts and Sciences into the very stone of the pillars to protect them from flood and fire.

In the early days of Freemasonry, these columns were represented at a lodge meeting by outlines in chalk on the door. As Masons became more condant and the need for clandestine meetings in temporary accommodation fell away, the columns became part of the furnishings of the lodge. Sometimes miniature replicas were held in the hands of the Senior and Junior Wardens. If the lodge was wealthy enough, huge ornate pillars would decorate the entrance.

The Temple of Solomon
destroyed by the Babylonians

THE TEMPLE OF SOLOMON

The most significant motif in Masonic symbolism is the use of the building of the Temple of Solomon as an allegory for perfecting the human individual. In Masonic legends the Temple was left unfinished because of the murder of the Architect Hiram Abiff. The actual Temple however was certainly finished and is described in almost laborious detail in the Old Testament. Biblical scholars and archaeologists have put the date when construction was begun at 957 BC, four years into his reign.

High walls of timber and stone surrounded an inner courtyard, which in turn surrounded the Temple itself, which consisted of an outer hallway, a main sanctuary reached through the two pillars which stood either side of the porchway entrance, and the Holy of Holies, the inner sanctum where the Ark of the Covenant was set.

The main sanctuary was lit by light from windows in the walls. The floor was decked out in cypress wood and the walls with cedar, overlaid with gold. However the inner sanctum, laid out as a perfect square, was windowless.

PYRAMID BUILDERS

Surrounding the Temple but with no direct access to it, were side chambers arranged on three storeys, which in Craft Masonry represent the three levels of initiation.

Unfortunately the original Temple was destroyed by King Nebuchadnezzar II in 586 BC. A second Temple was built in the sixth century BC, restored by the Maccabees and later by Herod the Great, but in 70 AD that too was demolished by the Romans. Under the Roman emperor Julian in 362 AD there was an attempt to rebuild it but this was abandoned and all that remains of the Temple is the retaining wall known as the Wailing Wall and the site is dominated by the resplendent gold dome of the Dome of the Rock.

One of the most enduring and indeed romantic myths surrounding Freemasons is that they were there at the building of the great pyramids at Giza. This is of course impossible to prove but there are similarities in Freemasonry to the ritual "journey through the chambers of the Pyramid" which has been deciphered by Egyptologists from hieroglyphs on the pyramid walls.

Much has been made in Masonic lore of the architect of the first stepped pyramid at Saqqara, known as Imhotep, chief architect to King Zoser. He was especially popular among French Freemasons after Napoleon invaded Egypt and all sorts of artefacts began to find their way back to France. An obsession with all things Egyptian soon gripped the nation and the myths and legends were incorporated into contemporary Masonic lore.

Of particular interest, because it echoed the story of Hiram Abiff, was the myth of Osiris, killed by his brother Seth and brought back to life by his sister-wife Isis. Nowadays Masonic lodges are replete with ancient Egyptian symbolism.

The three pyramids at Giza: Khufu, Khafre and Menkure

THE PYRAMID AND THE ALL - SEEING EYE

The All-seeing Eye atop the pyramid stands for the Great Architect or Supreme Being which is sometimes represented by the letter G. It can be found on the American dollar bill and many conspiracy theorists see this as proof that the most powerful country in the world is run by an elite body of Freemasons.

The Eye signifies that the Deity sees everything, even inside the Mason's soul and no bad deed goes unpunished, no matter how long karma may take to effect divine justice. The Egyptian influence is at work here too as the All-seeing Eye is a direct descendent of the Eye of Horus, which was ripped out by Seth and then healed by Thoth, the God of wisdom.

It is also known as the Eye of Providence and on the dollar bill appears surrounded by the Blaze of Glory, representing the divine source of creation. If you look closely you will see that there are thirteen steps, which represent the original thirteen states of the new nation. The pyramid, like the Temple of Solomon is unfinished.

Despite the fact that there were no Masons among the designers of the Great Seal of the United States, the rumors of Masonic involvement will not die out and the Latin inscriptions "Annuit Coeptus... It is favorable to our undertakings..." and "Novus Ordo Seclorum... A New Secular Order..." have been taken as signs that the Freemasons are intent on world domination.

Annuit Coeptis: "He (God) has favored our undertakings", (part of the great seal of the United States, usually seen on the back of a U.S one dollar bill)

THE SPHINX

Freemasons have also been linked with the building of the Sphinx that stands sentinel over the Great Pyramid at Giza and this composite figure has become an important Masonic symbol of the ineffable mystery of the Deity.

THE LABYRINTH

According to many Masonic legends, the architect who built the labyrinth for King Minos in Crete, where the dreaded Minotaur lurked, was a Freemason. The symbol of the labyrinth features heavily in Masonic ritual and is used to signify the arduous journey of the soul seeking enlightenment.

The Great Sphinx is believed to be the most immense stone sculpture ever made by man

The five noble orders of architecture

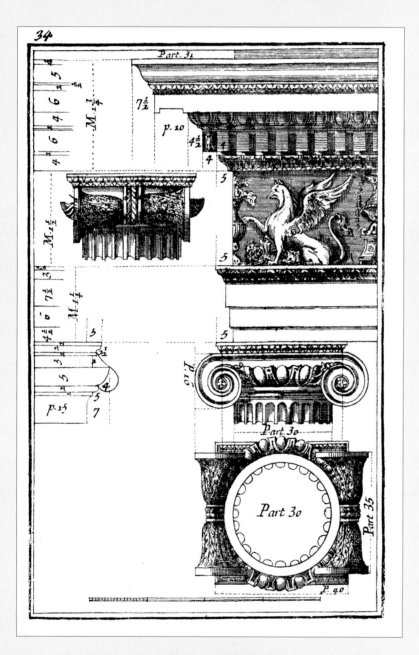

DORIC CAPITOL

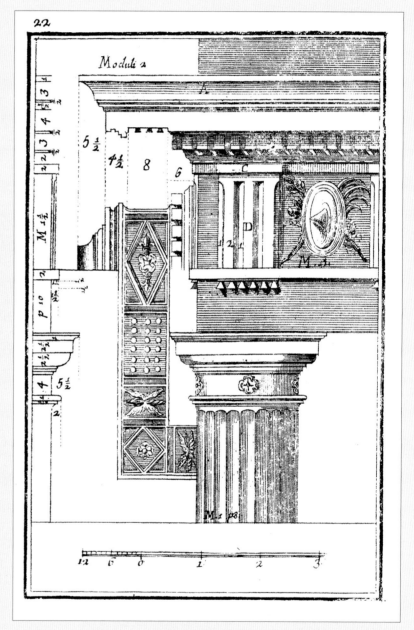

IONIC CAPITOL

Giacomo da Vignola (1507 - 1573), a theoretical and practical architect of the Transition Period between the Renaissance and Baroque styles, was the pupil and successor of Michelangelo. Born Giacomo Barozzi, in 1550 he was made papal architect by Pope Julius III.

His The Five Orders of Architecture (1563), became a standard work on the subject and was translated into many languages.

Based upon the work of Marcus Vitruvius Pollio (1st century BC), it undertook to formulate definite and minute rules for proportioning the classical orders appearing in the buildings of the Romans.

CORINTHIAN CAPITOL

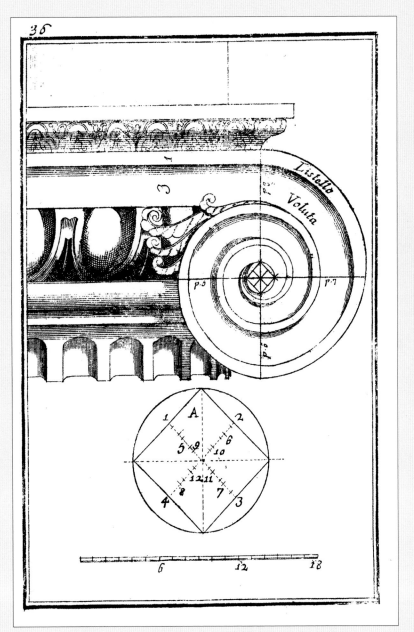

THE GOLDEN MEAN

  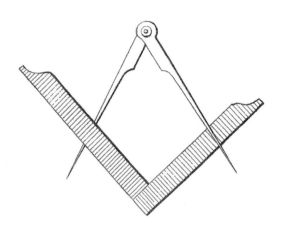

chapter 10

OW THAT FREEMASONRY HAS FALLEN INTO DISREPUTE, LARGELY AS A RESULT OF STEPHEN KNIGHT'S BOOK LINKING FREEMASONRY TO THE WHITECHAPEL MURDERS AS WELL AS SEVERAL PROMINENT SCANDALS AND ALLEGATIONS OF CORRUPTION, IT IS EASY TO FORGET THAT SOME OF THE MOST FAMOUS MEN AND THE BEST MINDS IN HISTORY WERE DEVOTED TO FREEMASONRY AND THE VIRTUES OF SELF-IMPROVEMENT AND FELLOWSHIP THAT IT ESPOUSED.

MEN FROM ALL WALKS OF LIFE HAVE TAKEN THE MASONIC OATH OF BROTHERHOOD: COMPOSERS, SCIENTISTS, LAW-MAKERS, POETS, PLAYWRIGHTS, ENGINEERS AND THERE HAVE EVEN BEEN MASONS ON THE MOON...

James VI and I, a keen advocate of Freemasonry, with his wife, Anne of Denmark

George Washington

Famous

PRESIDENTS OF THE UNITED STATES OF AMERICA

- George Washington, Fredericksburg Lodge No. 4; Alexandria Lodge No. 22, VA.
- James Monroe, Williamsburgh Lodge No. 6, VA.
- Andrew Jackson, Harmony Lodge No. 1; Past Grand Master of Tennessee.
- James K. Polk, Columbia Lodge No. 31, TN.
- James Buchanan, Past Master of Lancaster Lodge No. 43, Lancaster, PA.
- Andrew Johnson, Greenville Lodge No. 119, TN.
- James A. Garfield, Magnolia Lodge No. 20, OH.
- William McKinley, Hiram Lodge No. 21, VA.
- Theodore Roosevelt, Matinecock Lodge No. 806, Oyster Bay, NY.
- William Howard Taft, Kilwinning Lodge No. 356, OH.
- Warren G. Harding, Marion Lodge No. 70, OH.
- Franklin Delano Roosevelt, Holland Lodge No. 8, NY.
- Harry S Truman, 33° Belton Lodge No. 450, Belton, MO; Past Grand Master of Missouri
- Gerald Ford, Columbia Lodge No. 3, Washington, DC.

Harry S. Truman

Paul Revere

PLAYERS IN THE AMERICAN WAR OF INDEPENDENCE

· Benedict Arnold, Hiram Lodge No. 1, New Haven, CT.

· John Blair, Williamsburg Lodge No. 6; Past Grand Master of Virginia.

· Chief Joseph Brant, Hiram's Cliftonian Lodge No. 47, Barton Lodge No. 6, Hamilton, ON.

· Benjamin Franklin, February 1731, St. John's Lodge of Philadelphia; Lodge at Tun Tavern, Philadelphia, PA; WM, Loge des Neuf Soeurs, Paris; Past Grand Master of Pennsylvania.

· John Hancock, Massachusetts Lodge No. 277, QC; St. Andrew's Lodge, Boston, MA .

· William Hooper, Hanover Lodge, Masonborough, NC.

· John Paul Jones, St. Bernards Lodge No. 122, Kirkudbright, Scotland.

· Rufus King, St John's Lodge, Newburyport, MA.

· General Rufus Putnam, Past Grand Master of Ohio.

· Paul Revere, St. Andrew's Lodge, Boston, MA; Grand Master of Massachusetts 1794-97.

· Baron von Steuben, Trinity Lodge No. 10, New York, NY.

· Richard Stockton, charter Master, St. John's Lodge, Princeton, NJ.

· George Walton, Solomon's Lodge No. 1, Savannah, GA.

· Joseph Warren, St. Andrew's Lodge, Boston, MA; Past Provincial Grand Master of Massachusetts.

Bejamin Franklin

Freemasons

Theodore Roosevelt

John Paul Jones

BARONS OF INDUSTRY

- André Citroën, Lodge La Philosophie Positive, France.
- Samuel Colt, St. John's Lodge, Hartford, CT.
- Eberhard Faber, Chancellor Walworth Lodge No. 271, New York, NY.
- Henry Ford, Palestine Lodge No. 357, Detroit, MI.
- Charles Hilton, William B. Warren Lodge No. 309, IL.
- Frank G. Hoover, William McKinley Lodge No. 431, OH.
- George Pullman, Renovation Lodge No. 97, Albion, NY.
- A. Philip Randolph, Joppa Lodge No. 55, NYC USA.
- James Mayer Rothschild , Initiated Oct. 24, 1802: Emulation Lodge No. 12, England.
- Nathan Mayer Rothschild, Emulation Lodge No. 12, England.

Henry Ford

MUSICIANS

- Louis Armstrong, Montgomery Lodge No. 18 PHA, NY.
- Johann Sebastian Bach, Lodge of Nine Muses No. 235, England.
- William "Count" Basie, Wisdom Lodge No. 102, Chicago, IL.
- Irving Berlin, Munn Lodge No. 190, New York, NY.
- Nat King Cole, Thomas Waller Lodge No. 49, Los Angeles, CA, PHA.
- Edward Kennedy "Duke" Ellington, Social Lodge No. 1, Washington, DC, PHA.
- Sir William S. Gilbert, Lodge St. Machar No. 54, Aberdeen, Scotland.
- Joseph Haydn, Lodge Zur Wahren Eintracht, Austria.
- Franz Liszt, Lodge Zur Einigkeit, Germany.
- Wolfgang Amadeus Mozart, Lodge Zur Woltatigkeit, Vienna; Lodge Zur Wahren Eintracht, Austria.
- Jean Sibelius, Suomi Lodge No. 1, Helsinki, Finland.
- Sir Arthur Sullivan, Past Grand Organist of the United Grand Lodge of England.

William "Count" Basie

ENTERTAINERS

· Cecil B. DeMille, Prince of Orange Lodge No. 16, NY.
· Douglas Fairbanks, Beverly Hills Lodge No. 528, CA.
· W.C. Fields, E. Coppee Mitchell Lodge No. 605, Philadelphia, PA.
· Clark Gable, Beverly Hills Lodge No. 528, CA.
· Arthur Godfrey, Acacia Lodge No. 18, Washington, DC.
· Oliver Hardy, Solomon Lodge No. 20, Jacksonville, Florida.
· Harry Houdini, Initiated Aug 21, 1923, St. Cecile Lodge No. 568, NYC.
· Sir Henry Irving, Jerusalem Lodge No. 44, London.
· Al Jolson, St. Cecile Lodge No. 568, NY.
· Harold Lloyd, Hamilton Lodge No. 535, Hollywood, CA.
· Louis B. Mayer, St. Cecile Lodge No. 568, New York, NY.
· Richard Pryor, Henry Brown Lodge No. 22.
· Peter Sellers, Chelsea Lodge No. 3098, London, England.
· Robert Pershing, Wadlow, Franklin Lodge No. 25, Alton, IL.
· Jack Warner, Mount Olive Lodge No. 506, Los Angeles, CA.
· John Wayne, Marion McDaniel Lodge No. 56, Tucson, AZ.

Harry Houdini

LAW ENFORCERS

· J. Edgar Hoover, 33°, Grand Cross. Federal Lodge No. 1, Washington, DC.
· John Marshall, Past Grand Master of Virginia.
· Earl Warren, Past Grand Master of California.

J. Edgar Hoover

SPORTS PERSONALITIES

· Jack Dempsey, Kenwood Lodge No. 800, Chicago, IL.
· Jack Johnson, Lodge Forfar and Kincardine No. 225, Dundee, Scotland.
· Sugar Ray Robinson, Joppa Lodge No. 55, NY, PHA.

Jack Dempsey

WRITERS

· Andrew Bell, Lodge St. David No. 36, Scotland.
· James Boswell, Master of Canongate Kilwinning Lodge.
· Robert Burns, Saint David's Lodge No. 2174, Tarbolton.
· Lord William Byron, Grand Master of the Grand Lodge of England (Moderns).
· Samuel Clemens (Mark Twain), Polar Star Lodge No. 79, St. Louis.
· Sir Arthur Conan Doyle, Phoenix Lodge No. 257, Southsea, Hampshire.
· Johann Wolfgang von Goethe, Lodge Amalia, Weimar.
· Rudyard Kipling, Hope and Perseverance Lodge No. 782. E.C., Lahore, India;
  founding member, The Builders of the Silent Cities Lodge No. 12, St. Omer, France.
· Gotthold Ephraim Lessing, Lodge Zu den Drei Goldenen Rosen.
· Alexander Pope, Lodge Goat-at-the-Foot-of-the-Haymarket No. 16, England.
· Aleksandr Pushkin, Lodge Ovid, Kischinev.
· Friedrich Schiller, Rudolstadt Lodge, Germany.
· Sir Walter Scott, Saint David Lodge No. 36, Scotland.
· Jonathan Swift, Lodge Goat-at-the-Foot-of-the-Haymarket No. 16,
  London, England.
· Anthony Trollope, Banagher Lodge No. 306, Ireland.
· Voltaire, (François-Marie Arouet), Raised 1778 Loge des Neuf Soeurs, France.
· Oscar Wilde, Apollo University Lodge No. 357, England.
· Sir P.G. Wodehouse, Jerusalem Lodge No. 197, England.

Sir Walter Scott

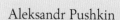

Aleksandr Pushkin

DAREDEVILS

- Edwin E. "Buzz" Aldrin, Clear Lake Lodge No. 1417, Seabrook, TX.
- Sir Richard Francis Burton, Hope Lodge, Kurrachee, Scinde, India.
- Admiral Richard E. Byrd, Federal Lodge No. 1, Washington, DC.
- Kit Carson, Montezuma Lodge No. 109, Taos, NM.
- William Clark, Saint Lewis Lodge No. 111, PA.
- Matthew Henson, Celestial Lodge No. 3, PHA, New York, NY.
- Meriwether Lewis, Door to Virtue Lodge No. 44, VA;
  founder, St. Louis Lodge No. 111, St. Louis, MO, under the Grand Lodge of Pennsylvania.
- Charles Lindbergh, Keystone Lodge No. 243, MO.
- Sir Robert Falcon Scott, Drury Lane Lodge No. 2127, London;
  Navy Lodge No. 2612, England.
- Sir Ernest Shackleton, Navy Lodge No. 2612, England.

Sir Ernest Shackleton

SCIENTISTS, AND INVENTORS

- Elias Ashmole, Warrington Lodge, England.
- Erasmus Darwin, St. David's Lodge No. 36, Scotland.
- John Theophilus Desaguliers, Past Grand Master of England.
- Richard Jordan Gatling, Centre Lodge No. 23, Indianapolis, IN.
- Joseph-Ignace Guillotin, founding member of the Grand Orient of France.
- Edward Jenner, Royal Berkeley Lodge of Faith and Friendship No. 449,
  Berkeley, England.
- Franz Mesmer, Lodge Les Philadelphes, France.
- Jacques-Étienne and Joseph-Michel Montgolfier, Loge des Neuf Soeurs, France.
- William Stukeley, Salutation Tavern Lodge, England.
- Sir Christopher Wren, Lodge of Antiquity No. 2, England.

Sir Christopher Wren

BRITISH ARISTOCRACY

· Prince Arthur, Duke of Connaught and Strathearn,
  Grand Master of the United Grand Lodge of England.
· HRH Prince Edward, Duke of Kent,
  Grand Master of the United Grand Lodge of England.
· Prince Michael of Kent, Grand Master of the Grand Lodge of Mark Master Masons.
· HRH Prince Edward Augustus, Duke of Kent and Strathearn,
  Grand Master of the Atholl or Antient Grand Lodge of England.
· HM King Edward VII, previously Grand Master of United Grand Lodge of England;
  Protector of the Craft.
· HM King Edward VIII, Household Brigade Lodge No. 2614;
  Past Grand Master of the United Grand Lodge of England.
· Andrew Bruce, 11th Earl of Elgin, Past Grand Master Mason of Scotland.
· HM King George IV, previously Grand Master of the Grand Lodge of England (Moderns),
  Grand Patron of UGLE from 1814.
· HM King George VI, Naval Lodge No. 2612; Past Grand Master of Scotland;
  Past Grand Master of the United Grand Lodge of England.
· HRH Prince Henry Frederick, Duke of Cumberland and Strathearn,
  Grand Master of the Grand Lodge of England (Moderns).

King Edward VII

PICTURE CREDITS

P. 1 Grand Lodge of British Columbia and Yukon. P. 7 Grand Lodge of British Columbia and Yukon. P. 8 Dover Publications. P. 9 Grand Lodge of British Columbia and Yukon. P. 10 Historical Picture Library. P. 11 Grand Lodge of British Columbia and Yukon. P. 12 The Stapleton Collection. P. 13 t: iStockphoto.com. b: Grand Lodge of British Columbia and Yukon. P. 14 t: Dover Publications. b: iStockphoto. P. 15 tl: Dover Publications. tr & b: Historical Picture Library. P. 16 Historical Picture Library. P. 17 Historical Picture Library. P. 18 Grand Lodge of British Columbia and Yukon. P. 19 Grand Lodge of British Columbia and Yukon. P. 20 Historical Picture Library. P. 21 Historical Picture Library. P. 22 t: Historical Picture Library. b: Grand Lodge of British Columbia and Yukon. P. 23 t: Library of Congress b: Historical Picture Library. P. 24/25 The Stapleton Collection. P. 27 Historical Picture Library. P. 28/29 Grand Lodge of British Columbia and Yukon. P. 30 iStockphoto.com. P. 31 Grand Lodge of British Columbia and Yukon. P. 32 t: Dover Publications. b: Historical Picture Library. P. 33 Dover Publications. P. 34/35 The Stapleton Collection. P. 36/37 Grand Lodge of British Columbia and Yukon. P. 38/39 Grand Lodge of British Columbia and Yukon. P. 40/41 The Stapleton Collection. P. 42 Grand Lodge of British Columbia and Yukon. P. 43 The Stapleton Collection. P. 44 Grand Lodge of British Columbia and Yukon. P. 47 The Stapleton Collection. P. 48 Grand Lodge of British Columbia and Yukon. P. 49 Grand Lodge of British Columbia and Yukon. P. 50/51 Grand Lodge of British Columbia and Yukon. P. 52 kena.org. P. 53 Dover Publications. P. 54/55 Grand Lodge of British Columbia and Yukon. P. 56 The Stapleton Collection. P. 57 Grand Lodge of British Columbia and Yukon. P. 58 t: Dover Publication. b: Historical Picture Library. P. 59 b: Dover Publication. P. 60 Dover Publication. P. 61 Historical Picture Library. P. 62/63 Dover Publication. P. 64 Historical Picture Library. P. 65 Historical Picture Library. P. 66 Dover Publication. P. 67 Historical Picture Library. P. 68 Historical Picture Library. P. 69 Historical Picture Library. P. 70/71 The Stapleton Collection. P. 72 Dover Publication. P. 73 iStockphoto.com P. 74 P. 75 Historical Picture Library. P. 76 Historical Picture Library. P. 77 Dover Publication. P. 78/79 Grand Lodge of British Columbia and Yukon. P. 80 The Stapleton Collection. P. 81 Grand Lodge of British Columbia and Yukon. P. 82 t: Dover Publication. b: Historical Picture Library. P. 83 Dover Publication. P. 84 Dover Publication. P. 86 Dover Publication. P. 88/89 The Stapleton Collection. P. 91 Dover Publication. P. 92/93 The Stapleton Collection. P. 94 Historical Picture Library. P. 95 Historical Picture Library. P. 96 Library of Congress. P. 97 Grand Lodge of British Columbia and Yukon. P. 98/99 Grand Lodge of British Columbia and Yukon. P. 100 Alexander Rose Visual Communications. P. 101 Grand Lodge of British Columbia and Yukon. P. 102 The Vatican Library. P. 103 iStockphoto.com. P. 104 iStockphoto.com. P. 106 Historical Picture Library. P. 107 istockphoto.com. P. 108 presstock.com P. 109 The Vatican Library. P. 110 The Vatican Library. P. 111 presstock.com P. 113 Alexander Rose Visual Communications. P. 114/115 Grand Lodge of British Columbia and Yukon. P. 116 iStockphoto.com. P. 117 Grand Lodge of British Columbia and Yukon. P. 118 iStockphoto.com. P. 119 nationalarchives.gov.uk. P. 120 T: ilnpictures.co.uk. b: nationalarchives.gov.uk. P. 121 c: ilnpictures.co.uk. b: London Metropolitan Archives. P. 122 t: nationalarchives.gov.uk. b: ilnpictures.co.uk. P. 123 t: nationalarchives.gov.uk. b: ilnpictures.co.uk. P. 124 t: ilnpictures.co.uk. c: nationalarchives.gov.uk. P. 125 iStockphoto.com. P. 126/127 Grand Lodge of British Columbia and Yukon. P. 128 The Stapleton Collection. P. 129 Grand Lodge of British Columbia and Yukon. P. 132 Historical Picture Library. P. 134/135 The Stapleton Collection. P. 138 The Stapleton Collection. P. 143 Grand Lodge of British Columbia and Yukon. P. 144/145 Grand Lodge of British Columbia and Yukon. P. 146 The Stapleton Collection. P. 147 Grand Lodge of British Columbia and Yukon. P. 148 t: Historical Picture Library. b: Library of Congress. P. 149 Dover Publication. P. 150 The Stapleton Collection. P. 152 Grand Lodge of British Columbia and Yukon. P. 153 Dover Publication. P. 154 Grand Lodge of British Columbia and Yukon. P. 156/157 The Stapleton Collection. P. 158 Grand Lodge of British Columbia and Yukon. P. 159 Grand Lodge of British Columbia and Yukon. P. 161 Dover Publication. P. 163 Historical Picture Library. P. 164 The Stapleton Collection. P. 165 Historical Picture Library. P. 167 Dover Publication. P. 168/9 Grand Lodge of British Columbia and Yukon. P. 170 The Stapleton Collection. P. 171 Grand Lodge of British Columbia and Yukon. P. 172/173 iStockphoto.com P. 174 Historical Picture Library. P. 175 iStockphoto.com P. 176 Alexander Rose Visual Communications. P. 177 Dover Publication. P. 178/179 Grand Lodge of British Columbia and Yukon. P. 180/181 Grand Lodge of British Columbia and Yukon. P. 182 The Stapleton Collection. P. 183 Grand Lodge of British Columbia and Yukon. P. 184/187 Library of Congress. P. 188 t: Library of Congress. c & b: Historical Picture Library. P. 189 Library of Congress. P. 190 Library of Congress.

Every effort has been made to obtain permission to reproduce copyright material, but there may be cases where we have ben unable to trace a copyright holder. The publisher will be happy to correct any omissions in future printings.

Images are listed from the top (t = top, tr = top right, tl = top left, c = center, b = bottom).